HOW TO SELF PUBLISH YOUR OWN BOOK

AND MAKE IT A BEST SELLER

by

TED NICHOLAS

First Printing - October, 1975

Second Printing (Revised) - September 1976

Library of Congress Number - 75-33601
ISBN - 0-913864-11-0

Published by
ENTERPRISE PUBLISHING COMPANY
1300 Market Street
Wilmington, Delaware 19801

TABLE OF CONTENTS

TABLE OF CONTENTS

Page

TABLE OF CONTENTS

HOW TO SELF PUBLISH YOUR OWN BOOK

AND MAKE IT A BEST SELLER

by

TED NICHOLAS

<u>FOREWORD</u>

As an author interested in self publishing you have knocked on the door of one of our most mysterious institutions: Publishing.

The mystery is no accident. But this book will take you inside, introduce you to the methodology, terminology and techniques. It will explain why fewer than one-tenth of one percent of authors self publish.

Most important, as an author who has self published two best sellers and sold over 125,000 books, I'll explain the entire process in terms the lay author understands. I wasn't born into publishing. I learned it. And through this book I'll demonstrate to you not only the techniques of self publishing, but also the essentials of advertising and promotion necessary to make your book a best-selling success.

For openers you may be interested in a fact that I hadn't known until I published my own work, namely, <u>conventional best seller lists are a myth</u>.

My book, "How to Form Your Own Corporation Without a Lawyer for Under $50", has been among the top 10 non-fiction sellers in the U. S. for over 2 years. Yet it has never appeared on a best seller list. Many readers buy a book only because it is on a "Best Seller" list. Naturally, I wanted mine listed. However, when

NOTE: This entire book is prepared in the form of a manuscript to serve as an example of how your book should be organized and typed.

I queried several nationally distributed newspapers and one smaller one I learned that their best seller lists are assembled exclusively from bookstore reports. While my books sell well in bookstores, the largest sales volume comes from mail order buyers. I was informed that mail order books, accounting for an estimated 40% of all books sold in the U.S., were not even considered!

There are other popular myths about the publishing industry.

Most writers, both beginners as well as known and experienced ones, believe that writing a book is at least 90 percent of the task of selling it to the book buyer. I submit that the writing of any book is, at most, 10 percent of the task. Selling it to the book buyers of the world is the other 90 percent.

Prior to its printing, your manuscript is a creative, artistic embryo, but once off the press, it becomes a product. And unless you want copies for no other reason than to stack in your basement, your book must be treated as a product. Thousands of well written books on a variety of valuable subjects are gathering dust in warehouses because the sales effort was inadequate or non-existent For that reason a large portion of this book is devoted to promotion and sales.

I want to dispel several myths about the publishing
industry which have tended to cause authors to shy away from self
publishing. The first involves costs. (Most people think it costs
many thousands of dollars to publish a book.) That's simply not so.
I'm going to show you how to do it step by step for less than $1000,
or about a dollar a copy to print.

Myth #2. (My book doesn't have a chance to succeed without
many thousands spent on advertising and promotion.) I'll show you
how to test the market for your book before you've invested a dime
in getting it printed using the same market research techniques
large publishing houses spend millions on each year. The secret
lies with rifling low cost classified ads into carefully selected
publications. I'll tell you what to say and where to say it.

I'll also explode some myths about the use of television
in promoting your book after it is published. Rather than a closed
avenue for the new author, TV talk shows provide a very real
opportunity for the newly published writer to discuss his work.
Remember, once you've published a book, you are immediately regarded
as an authority on your subject. It's an almost magical threshold
you pass over once your name appears as the author on a printed
volume. I have promoted my books on some of the nation's largest
television and radio shows without cost to me. I'll tell you who to
contact and how to go about it.

Finally, as the promotion of your book begins to create a demand for it, the results will begin to blend. Your ads and individual promotions will provide you with new material for other ads such as "Ted Nicholas, who has appeared on TV and radio," or "This new book was reviewed by San Francisco Chronicle, who said this about it ...." At that point others are promoting you. If you approach the matter of publishing your book as a series of tasks that must be done, the reward could be a conventional publisher coming to you with an attractive proposal.

A long shot? The odds are enormously better than getting published as an unknown author by a large publisher.

Your reasons for wanting a book published with your name on it can be varied. For many doctors, lawyers and teachers a published book helps enhance professional status. To business executives it can pave the way for job promotions. Other authors want financial success from their literary efforts.

Some writers are not interested in getting involved with the sales and business side of publishing. This is, of course, their choice, although in my view they miss most of the fun.

However, many writers cannot get their work published at all or they are dissatisfied with previous arrangements or the lack of sales effort. Others would love to be involved with all the steps that are necessary to place their book in the hands of as

many readers as they are able. After all, no one is as interested
as you are in your book's success.

You will be shown how to handle the entire publishing
project for your book with samples of successful methods that are
proven.

If you have or plan to prepare a marketable book, there
will be facts and ideas to put you on the path of accomplishment,
notoriety and financial rewards. Some of you will become wealthy.
Others who simply want to experience the thrill of seeing your work
in print, will now be able to do so at minimum cost.

This book offers you an alternative that makes it
possible for you to accomplish what may be impossible any other
way -- your own self published best seller.

OPTIONS

Conventional Publishers

On any given day in New York City an estimated 100,000 manuscripts sit gathering dust in the files of various publishers. With 350,000 books written each year and only 40,000 printed, the odds of an unknown author's first book seeing print at a conventional publishing house are highly against him.

Out of the ones that are published, over 90% do not sell out their first printing. The average number of books in an initial printing is only 5,000 copies. Neither the writer, who usually receives a royalty of 5% to 15%, or the publisher earn much money, or gain notoriety, if either is a goal.

From your point of view as a writer who may not be well known, the odds of your book being published are 10 to 1 against you. The odds are also 10 to 1 against your book selling out the first printing. And the odds are infinitesimally small that you will sell the tens of thousands of copies necessary to earn the description "best seller".

Looking at those odds can be very discouraging to the aspiring writer. Often it takes long months, frequently years of effort to write a book. Then to have it not published or handled poorly by a publisher can be anguishing.

Conventional, or "risk" publishers are in business to make money. In order for a large publisher to break even on a book, it must sell a minimum of 5,000-10,000 copies. In order to reduce their risks, these large publishing houses seek out known authors. They then invest in advertising to virtually guarantee profitable sales. Even in these cases very few books sell beyond 20,000 copies in hard cover editions. Publishers hope to make the largest profits in later pickup by book clubs, and finally transition to a low cost paperback. Sometimes there are also movie rights to a book that can be profitably sold.

Surprisingly, large publishers seldom spend more than $50,000 in advertising and promotion even for a best seller. In one year, 1973, I spent in excess of $350,000 in advertising on my first book. The best part is that it was accomplished with little risk, on a pay as you go basis.

Unknown authors, regardless of the quality of their books, are avoided by conventional publishers. One way around the problem is to self publish, self promote and create a product that will be sought out by publishers. My book, "How to Form Your Own Corporation Without a Lawyer for Under $50," held no interest for the large publishers I approached with the manuscript in 1972. However, after

I had written, promoted, advertised and sold over 100,000 copies, no less than nine major publishing houses have since made offers to buy hard cover and paperback rights to the book.

Of course, now there is little incentive for me to share the profits with anyone else. I was fortunate to realize early in my publishing career that no one is as interested in an author's work as the author himself.

The strangest phenomenon I have witnessed is the reluctance authors feel about promoting their book themselves. Most simply choose not to become involved. What they lose in the process is their greatest chance at success.

One writer (a prominent judge) told me recently of his experience with his first book. It was well written and an exciting book in my opinion. It was published by one of the largest and best known publishers. After two years of unimpressive sales, he visited the publisher to learn what was being done to promote and advertise his work. He wanted to see the file. To his amazement they had never done any promotion, so there was no such file. Needless to say he is not having them publish his next book.

I am not suggesting that all writers have bad experiences with their publishers. There are some who generally are pleased with their publisher's performance. However, the worst factor about arrangements between author and publisher is that they nearly always favor the publisher. The writer loses control over the destiny of his book after publication. He also must give up all future rights to his work.

If your book doesn't sell by itself, the chance of it getting much advertising support from a large publisher is slight. A large publisher has hundreds of books to sell. It cannot and does not heavily promote each one. Such establishments work on the premise that a few of the many titles will sell enough copies to pay the overhead of the entire publishing operation. Occasionally a book sells without much publicity or fanfare through its "word of mouth" reputation, but it is an exceptional feat.

My final suggestion about conventional publishers is that you should contact them. If you beat the odds, and they are interested in your work, ask to talk with other authors publishing with the house. Then ask yourself how much control you are willing to give up. With those answers you will be prepared to make your best judgment.

Vanity Publishers

Authors discouraged by the high odds against publication of their work by conventional publishers are frequently seduced by advertisements which appear in the back of all literary magazines and some consumer publications. They read "Manuscripts Wanted ..." These ads are placed by vanity or subsidy publishers who too frequently promise more than they deliver.

The typical scenario sees the author packing off his manuscript to the address indicated in the ad. A few days later he receives a glowing "review" indicating that the book has great potential for success.

With the author's ego sufficiently massaged, the vanity publisher follows up with a contract which promises royalty payments to the author of 40 percent of sales so long as he is willing to pay the cost of the first printing of the book. The kicker is that the contract carefully avoids any guarantee of sales. And, in fact, the vanity publisher doesn't expect any appreciable sales. He makes his money in the printing costs alone. The best tipoff is that no conventional publisher could or would promise 40 percent royalty payments on a book that was to be adequately promoted. Those royalties typically average 5-15 percent.

Since printing is the real livelihood of the vanity publisher, he is virtually uninterested in the aspects of publishing that affect sales of a book, namely editing, advertising and promotion, and sales.

Editing represents a cost to the vanity publisher, and since he expects no potential return from sales, he gives only the slightest attention to this important phase. Gross spelling and grammatical errors are corrected, but little else.

Printing and binding charges generally run several thousand dollars with a vanity publisher -- considerably more than a similar self-publishing effort would cost. Furthermore, frequent practice is to bind a few copies for the author while the bulk of the edition is neither bound nor ever distributed.

A vanity publisher's contract usually provides for promotion to consist of review copies, advertising and bookstore distribution.

Review copies, sent as promised to editors of book review media, are almost automatically tossed out without reading more than the name of the publishing house. The name alone, to an experienced reviewer is enough to tip him off to a vanity book that probably isn't worth his valuable time to read.

The advertising most vanity publishers do is just enough to fulfill the terms outlined in the contract. The most popular technique is to "tombstone" many titles in a classified ad in the New York Times. Such an advertising method by itself is almost as inexpensive as it is ineffective.

As for bookstore distribution, few bookstores will stock a vanity book since there is almost never a demand. The exception might be as a favor to a local author.

Vanity publishers do serve as a means to get a book into print. Depending upon your own desires, they may or may not be the best way. If you simply want to see your book in print and are not particularly concerned about price or promotion after printing, then a vanity publisher could be for you.

The prime caveat is, read the contract and understand the terms. Don't let the heady glow of apparent acceptance dull your judgment. Also, call the Better Business Bureau to help to determine the business reputation of the vanity publisher.

Do It Yourself

Self publishing is neither new (Shelley, Walt Whitman and William Blake did it); nor is it unique (there are an estimated 500 authors today who have self published); nor is it unsuccessful (as previously mentioned, I have sold over 125,000 books at prices of $7.95 to $14.95 this way).

Many authors came to self publish for the reason Mark Twain did. He was discouraged with his relationship with conventional publishers. As a result, he self published Huckleberry Finn. Other authors, like Upton Sinclair, were unable to get their first books accepted by conventional publishers. He paid to have his first novel printed.

Still other authors like Zane Grey came to self publishing through totally unrelated but successful vocations. Grey was a dentist in Ohio. The publishers he submitted his first novel to opined he ought to stay a dentist. He brought out Betty Zane in 1904 and shortly thereafter gave up the tooth repair profession altogether.

Other authors you will recognize also self published such as Carl Sandburg, Ezra Pound, James Joyce and D. H. Lawrence. Joyce's Ulysses was too long, they said. And Lawrence's Lady Chatterly's Lover was too dirty. History obviously proved that conventional publishers are not omniscient.

Most important, self publishing is not difficult, at least not in the sense that an average author can't do it. It does take work, just like writing a book does. Most of all, it takes persistence.

You don't need printing presses, a staff of editorial pros, proofreaders, or a battery of advertising agents. Like a person who sub-contracts the building of his house, you simply buy the time and effort of printers, editors, proofreaders and advertising agents as you need them. And many of the jobs you can do yourself.

Perhaps the most easily overlooked benefit of self publishing is that you retain control over your work. That factor becomes increasingly important if your book is even moderately successful in sales.

Methods of Self Publishing

If you are on a tight or non-existent budget, find a small printing firm willing to print the book in exchange for royalties to come. They absorb the printing costs and they receive 5-15 percent royalties on your sales.

Another no cost arrangement is based upon finding a printer to print the book and sell it. You, the author, receive payment in actual copies of the printed book itself. For example, 10 percent of a press run of 500 books would net you 50 books. Thus, as the author, you see the work in print and have sufficient copies to send to reviewers and select promotional media members.

Perhaps too frequently writers share three characteristics: misery, obscurity and poverty. However, what one writer is unable to do alone, a group can sometimes pull off. An example of such a cooperative arrangement between two writers exists in the Magic Circle Press, a publishing house created by Adele Aldridge and a partner who put up $1000 apiece to get their own poetry, prose and art into print. They published a work entitled Not Poems which they sell for $3.50. Magic Circle has printed 3,000 copies and received $5,400 in income. Expenses for paper, printing and binding came to $2,951. Mailing envelopes were $59; promotion $300 and postage $400. The net profit thus far is $1,690 but includes much of their own free editorial labor.

Self publishing can take many forms depending upon your assets, interests and your abilities. I would now like to outline the step by step process I used to publish and promote my own works.

STEP BY STEP

Choosing a Subject

The first step in self publishing your own best selling book is to choose a subject with high sales potential. It must have mass market appeal if your goal is to exceed even 10,000 in sales. A recent study by Doubleday revealed that the subject -- not the author's name or reviewer's comments -- was the key to a successful book. The subjects with the best sales potential in this country are money, sex, health, psychological well being, hobbies, "How to's" and, of course, fiction. Unless you are not interested in large sales, it is best to avoid "protest" subjects or others with built in audience limitations.

As a publisher I am constantly surprised at the large number of people who have valuable information in their heads, but simply do not think in terms of sharing it with others through publication of a book. The book buying public is willing to pay handsomely for valuable information, and this is a key to pricing your book, a topic I'll discuss at some length a little later.

Preparing the Manuscript

Doctors, businessmen, auto mechanics or housewives, and hundreds of thousands of other people write books each year and have them published. All obviously are not professional writers, and they needn't be. Nor do you need to be.

The information you have to offer the public is what buyers are willing to pay for. But how do you get that information on paper if you aren't a skilled writer? The most effective method I've found is to place a classified ad in the local paper for editorial help in preparing a book. Newspapermen, public relations people, advertising workers, librarians and a host of others have skills which you can purchase on a part time basis to help organize your thoughts and your material. You might need help only to get a working outline, then use a tape recorder to fill in the information.

A librarian is a natural person to contact for help in researching your work, again on a part time basis. Most librarians also have a good working command of the English language and can put research findings into usable final form.

If the writing process is foreign to you and you want to avoid it altogether, you can advertise for a "ghostwriter." Be sure to see samples of his work, and agree on a method of payment. A simple working contract can be sketched out stating what he will be paid, and that all revenue from sale of the book will be yours. Also, that it will be published under your name.

Once the manuscript is out of the draft stage and edited, you can hire a typist to prepare it "camera-ready." If typed without errors on an IBM Correcting Selectric II* typewriter using a carbon ribbon, your manuscript can be photocopied by a printing platemaker saving hundreds or even thousands of dollars in type-setting and printing costs. The book you are reading was prepared using this method combined with photo offset printing. Before you prepare the final manuscript, contact a printer and discuss the specific details with him.

Let me offer a final note regarding manuscripts. As a publisher of other authors' works, I receive many original manu-

* Outside the U.S. the Swiss made Hermes is an excellent choice.

scripts in the mail. My advice is to retain your original manuscript in all cases, and to store it in a fireproof box. I won't say publishers are careless, but they are human, just like mailmen. So long as you provide a legible duplicate, there is no reason to submit an original to a publisher or a printer.

Writing for the Reader

A book about creating a bestseller wouldn't be complete without some tips on the process of putting words and sentences together to form a communications unit. There is no magic formula so far as I know. But the best writing is always simple, clear and understandable. Shoot for those goals in your work.

Here are 14 suggestions that are generally accepted among successful writers in the English language:

1. Avoid the temptation to use a big word when a small one will do better. Try to write like you speak. Surveys show that the average person's vocabulary ranges from 800 to 1000 words. With some 26,000 English words you can see how easy it is to stray into areas of the unknown with your readers.

2. The purpose of writing is to communicate, not to impress.

3. Use simple, declarative sentences.

4. Before you begin to write, read a few pages of a writer's work you admire. Don't consciously copy another's style, that won't work. Instead, let your subconscious help you make editorial decisions as you write.

5. Use the precise word to express just the meaning you want.

6. Vary sentence length.

7. Avoid colloquial words and phrases. Also avoid jargon or an excess of technical language unless your subject demands it. Most don't.

8. Use action verbs and nouns which tend to call up a mental picture for the reader. Put sight, smell and taste into your writing.

9. Avoid overuse of adverbs and adjectives. They are too often imprecise in meaning. Avoid superlatives. Avoid descriptions like "very big."

10. Vary paragraph length, but strive for short paragraphs in the main.

11. Don't overuse the word "I" in your copy.

12. Put the words you want to emphasize in the beginning of a sentence. Put the sentence you want to emphasize at the beginning of a paragraph. Put the paragraph you want to emphasize at either the beginning or end of a chapter.

13. Revise. Revise. Revise. Cut words which do not add to your message. Your writing can always be tightened, improved.

14. Writing is hard work most of the time. If you're doing it correctly, writing will give you a good intellectual and emotional workout; although it is also probably among the most rewarding forms of productive work in which you can engage.

Choosing and Testing the Title

The importance of a title for a potential best seller is perhaps the most frequently disregarded fact in publishing. An author might spend years agonizing over his manuscript only to sit down over a cup of coffee with the publisher to decide on a title.

The very best way to sell self published books is by direct mail. It is the method of exposing your work to the widest possible audience for the fewest initial dollars invested in promotion. You can start small and pyramid your profits to larger and larger advertising programs. Thus the importance of a title becomes clear. It must grab the reader's attention and offer him information that will benefit him.

Since a title is of such importance in mail order book

merchandising, I have developed a technique of title testing which costs very little, but provides solid market research data both for title selection as well as further advertising.

Let's say you have written a book on Organic Gardening, a subject of widespread interest today. How do you choose a title? Perhaps the "How to" approach, giving rise to something like "How to Grow a More Productive Garden." Or perhaps, "Secrets of Organic Gardening" would be better?

To test the pulling power of these titles you need do nothing more than place a classified ad in one or more gardening magazines. If you choose a publication which specializes in one facet of gardening, it will probably have a lower circulation figure than one dealing with the entire gardening gamut. And ad rates will be correspondingly lower in the smaller circulation magazine.

What should your ad say? It ought to read something like this: "New book being completed called 'How to Grow a More Productive Garden.' For free information write to ..."

What's the free information? For about $12 per thousand you can have an 8½" x 11" circular printed to contain the pertinent information about your book. It would include all the titles you are testing, so you can use the same circular to respond to inquiries from all your ads. Vary the titles in the ads to test the pulling power of each.

The circular should also contain the table of contents of your book.

In addition, the respondent can be offered a financial inducement to purchase a copy of your book when it's hot off the press. Perhaps here you say something like, "As a pre-publication offer I would be happy to autograph your copy of my new book and give you a two dollar discount from the advertised retail price. It will be off the press in 60 days!"

Finally the circular should contain a coupon enabling a person to order easily. You will always receive more orders if you stress a prompt money back guarantee in the event someone did not like the book.

You will find that some checks will begin to flow in before your book is even printed. And at this point you can begin to analyze several things: 1) The title which brings in the greatest number of inquiries (one almost always dramatically outpulls others) and 2) your "conversion rate" -- the number of people who write for the free information and then go on to purchase the book. It's also possible you will receive enough advance orders to pay for the printing costs.

Of course, the book at this point has not even been printed. And you haven't invested money in printing a book with an ineffective title. Plus you have gained a good feel for the potential market acceptance of your book with an investment of less than $50. If your title is effective, and the book is priced right, you should receive many times that amount in checks from people who take advantage of your pre-publication offer.

Pricing and Factors Affecting Pricing

Many myths exist in publishing regarding the pricing of books. It is my experience that when you are selling valuable information to people, the selling price is not nearly as frightening to a buyer as it is to the author. Publishers Weekly indicates that the average price for hardcover books in 1974 was $14.09 while quality paperbacks averaged $4.38. Writers tend to feel immoral selling a book for $10 if it only cost $1 to produce. That's why writers are so often poor, and publishers rich.

The concept that works most successfully in book sales is similar to the marketing practice used in cosmetics. A lipstick that sells for a dollar costs only pennies to make. However, a large portion of the difference goes into advertising. So it is with a self published book. Your selling price breakdown should be like this on a $10 book: $5 for advertising and promotion; $2 cost of production (printing, graphics, artwork); $3 for operating overhead and profit.

If there is a standard in the self publishing field, it probably has been a selling price of about twice production cost. This standard has undoubtedly accounted for many a self publishing failure. What it leaves out is the vital margin for advertising.

The type and style of book you produce directly affects the cost of producing it. The factors entering here are: size, number of pages, paper vs. hardcover, paper stock, quantity, illustrations.

Let's take them one at a time:

Size - Most books are printed in a 6x9 inch size, largely because it is the most economical. Each page will take about 400 words of 10 point type (about the size you are reading now). Other sizes are 3½"x6", 4½"x7" (paperback size) and 8½"x11". The 8½"x11" size is convenient when working from camera-ready copy typed on that size page. No photo-reduction or enlargement is required for platemaking. Type size is very readable and you will know exactly how the printed product will look even before publication. Small formats are

restrictive. They often do not fit right on book-
shelves, and they might be more expensive than the
6x9 inch size because of paper waste. Too large a
size is expensive and cumbersome and offers no
advantage except in reproducing large illustrations.

Paper or hardcover - Paperbacks are less costly by
up to $2 per book. They are also lighter and thus
cost less to mail. However, if you want to offer
a luxurious product, consider the clothbound hardcover. Remember, you can have both cloth and paperback editions of your book. You can always get 250
hardcovers and 750 paperbacks in a 1000 book run.
An 80 pound dust cover on colored stock will enhance
the sales appeal of a hardback book.

Paper stock - Generally a 50 pound weight is best
for paperbacks with covers printed on a heavier,
glossy kromekote sheet. For hardbacks, a 60 pound
sheet is preferred.

Other details such as type of binding, type
face, etc., can be discussed with your printer and
will depend somewhat upon his equipment and
capabilities.

Methods of Printing

Two printing methods account for almost all books produced today, letter press and photo offset. The older method, letter press, uses type cast in hot metal, then secured onto a plate which is placed onto a printing press. The printing occurs through an impression on the paper similar to a typewriter.

Letter press printing requires highly skilled, usually union tradesmen and is costly. The newer and cheaper method of printing is called photo offset. In simplest terms, a printing plate is made photographically from virtually any piece of printed material. For this reason, if you type a manuscript page on 8½"x11" paper, it can be photo-reduced to fit the 6"x9" page. You eliminate all typesetting costs in the process. An alternative to preparing the final "camera-ready" manuscript is to have type set by photo composition, or "cold type." This method is far less expensive than linotype (type cast in hot metal). Cold type offers literally thousands of different type faces and sizes, again, depending upon the printer's resources.

With cold type composition copy can be set by any competent typist using a composing machine which is frequently hooked into a computer. The procedure for showing proofs to the author is essentially the same for hot or cold type composition.

Customarily "first proofs" or "galley proofs" represent the first set copy the author receives to proofread. After corrections are noted, they are reset and second proofs shown.

In the offset process the subject to be reproduced (writing, typing, type, artwork, etc.) is transferred to a thin, flat offset printing plate. The offset plate is then mounted onto the plate cylinder of an offset press. During the operation the inked image of the plate is printed onto a rubber-covered surface of a cylinder which in turn transfers the image to the paper.

How Original Copy is Reproduced

The way this is done is to essentially take a photograph of the material to be reproduced. For example, to reproduce a typed page by photo offset, the printer or platemaker shoots a negative of the page. It will reproduce only 100% black (the type) and 100% white (all on the page which is not typed). This is called a "line shot."

The photo negative is made to the desired size of the final product. That is, it can be enlarged in proportion to its original size. Let's say you want to reproduce an 8½"x11" typed page. The negative then is made to 8½"x11" and it is transferred to a paper, plastic or metal printing plate which bears a light sensitive emulsion coating. Thus the negative image becomes positive on the plate. Then it is transferred to the printing blanket and reversed, only to become positive again when printed on the sheet.

In addition to "line" or solid black and white subjects, printers make "halftone" screens. The ink fountain of an offset press carries ink of a single tone of one color, for example, black. On the printed sheet of paper then, the press can print only solid black areas, or it can leave areas white. To give the illusion of printing a continuous tone, as exists in any photograph, a halftone screen is superimposed on the photo to be reproduced. The screen like a window screen, is made up of many tiny individual square sections. Each tiny square can be totally filled with ink, totally empty, or it can be partially inked. Totally filled would print solid black; totally empty, solid white; partially filled would print some shade of gray. Thus when you see a black and white photo reproduced in a magazine you are actually seeing a grid laid over the photo with some grids black, some white, and some gray. Look with a magnifying glass and you'll see it.

If you have photographs to be reproduced in your book, your printer will have the picture "screened" and show you proofs indicating how they will reproduce in the finished book.

With the addition of photographs the platemaking process becomes somewhat more complicated. The screened photos (or halftones) must be combined with the type (or line copy) in the same positions they will occupy in the finished page. They are "stripped" together into a "flat." The flat is a paper matrix with holes cut in where the line and halftone copy appear. The actual printing plate is made by exposing the plate's light sensitive surface through the holes in the flat.

Printing It Yourself

There is yet another avenue of printing open to the self publishing author. That is doing the whole job yourself.

Before rushing out to purchase a four color perfecting press, bear in mind that without a large capital outlay and considerable talent, printing is usually best left in the domain of the professional. However, if your book is to consist of text only (no illustrations or artwork) and the material lends itself to a simple binding method (preferably loose leaf) then do-it-yourself printing is a reasonable possibility. If the information you plan to publish needs to be updated frequently, a loose leaf type of binding might be ideal. Such a procedure also allows for additional sales of updated information to a very prime audience, your previous customers.

An acquaintance of mine began a "kitchen table" publishing house about two years ago that provided him a comfortable income while attending law school. Before deciding on law for his life's work, he had wanted to be a doctor. Upon applying to medical schools in this country he found only closed doors. One of his friends told him that many medical schools overseas had vacancies.

Despite my friend's change in vocations from medicine to law, he learned a great deal about medical school vacancies abroad. In what proved to be a wise entrepreneurial move, he decided to share his knowledge with other prospective medical students by publishing a book.

As a student he did not have sufficient capital to pay to have his book published, and he was the type of individual who enjoyed doing things himself. That combination of ingredients motivated him to buy a multilith press capable of handling a standard 8½"x11" sheet. He typed directly onto paper masters (printing plates) which attach to the press.

The book production process became a family affair with his wife punching holes in the sheets and assembling them in the proper sequence while he printed. The final steps were assembling them into three-hole binders and then shipping.

He was able to advertise his service by posting inexpensive notices on school bulletin boards. His operation was simple, but did not require any greater degree of sophistication than he was able to lend to it.

Types of Binding

Paperback books of fewer than 80 pages are usually saddle stitched by two staples in the center fold of the publication. Books with more pages are either glued or stapled together (Perfect bound) to form a square back. Then the paper cover can be glued on.

Clothbound books are usually either Smyth sewn with thread or else employ side stitch binding. These last longer and generally show less wear. They are, however, more expensive than Perfect binding.

There are various other bindings available if you prefer the unusual or offbeat approach. These can be discussed with your printer.

Perhaps the latest innovation in binding is a method called Velo-Bind. It shows promise for the self publishing author

because it is well suited to short press runs of even a few
hundred copies. Velo-Bind produces an inexpensive, square back,
permanent binding through use of hot-melt plastic to fasten pages
together. Then the cover is bonded to the rest of the book. It
is available from Velo-Bind Press of Sunnyvale, California.

Photos -- An Important Asset

Writers sometimes tend to think books should have words
only and leave pictures to the magazines. For a novel I'd probably
agree. But other books can benefit greatly from the use of photos.
Those on travel, beauty culture, and many how-to books would suffer
without photos to clearly define just what the writer is setting
out to show. A novelist, on the other hand, probably doesn't want
his characters visually defined except in the imaginations of the
readers.

If you feel your book would benefit by including photos,
you are immediately confronted with the problem of where to obtain
them. Here is a list of 10 places you can start.

1. You can hire free-lancers.

2. Prowl libraries, art galleries, and museums. Many
   have Ektachrome transparencies of paintings and
   exhibits available for free use.

3. Turn to other publications for help, either on a
   free or payment basis.

4. Buy from photo syndicates or supply houses
   who sell "stock" photos.

5. Seek assistance from your local Chamber of Commerce.

6. Check professional, trade, and industry associates for no-cost photos.

7. Private companies (usually through their public
   relations departments) will often provide free
   PR photos.

8. Contact government sources. Perhaps Department
   of Agriculture for gardening photos.

9. You can keep an eye open for photographers who
   might appear at an event that you are covering.
   Get their names; ask to see results; offer to
   buy if good.

10. Finally, take your own!

Taking Your Own Pictures

I would suggest you limit your photography to black and
white unless the subject specifically warrants the additional
expense of 4-color printing. (It will probably cost about four times
as much as a black and white book).

If you are not an accomplished photographer, here are some pointers on cameras. There are five types, and all except Polaroid will yield top quality negatives suitable for making prints to reproduce in your book.

1. The single-lens reflex with built in light meter. I like this type best. Popular makes are Argus, Pentax, Nikon, Canon and Alpha. Also 2¼x2¼ single-lens reflex cameras such as Japanese Bronica and Swedish Hasselblad. Advantages -- small, portable, sturdy, easy to operate, and a wide variety of lenses is available.

2. The 35mm rangefinder (you look at image through optical viewfinder). Leica makes the best.

3. Twin lens reflex -- one lens takes the picture; the second reflects image up to the eye by means of a mirror. Rolleiflex and Mamiya are most popular makes and 2¼x2¼ the usual negative size. Advantages -- permits photographer to see object on groundglass with total perspective, sharpness, and mood captured by the lens. Larger negative size permits big enlargements if needed. Limitations -- not many lens choices, "look down" sighting, a square format that makes composition tricky.

4. Press or view camera. These are outmoded, bulky, tough

to lug around, and impossible for candids. But the
large negative offers great enlargement potential.
Used mostly for studio work. Top cameras: Linhof,
Deardorff and Speed Graphic.

5. Polaroid. These are used by some pros to set up shots
for other cameras, but rarely for reproduction.

Avoid box cameras, subminiatures, or stereos. I would
suggest you buy the best camera you can afford. Standardize on
one type. Master it before thinking about expanding your equipment
inventory. The photographic end result lies about 75 percent with
the photographer and about 25 percent with his equipment.

Elements of a Good Photo

You will want the pictures you take to look "professional"
rather than snapshot-like. Here are some pointers to bear in mind
both when taking photos of your own, and in selecting photos others
have taken for possible inclusion in your book:

-- Avoid clutter and distracting elements that pull
the eye from the main point.

-- Seek ... contrast in pattern and tonal shades.

-- Seek ... action, either obvious or implied.

-- Tell a story. And remember, even a portrait can tell
    a story -- a smile, a scowl, an intense expression,
    a disdainful mood.

-- Seek ... unusualness. Unlike anything seen before.

-- Seek ... human interest and feeling.

-- Strive for technical perfection in focus, exposure
    and development.

    (Occasionally, blurred image or fuzzy focus can
    serve a purpose, but use the technique sparingly.)

Handling Photos

As a final note on using photos in your book, don't
ruin otherwise suitable pictures by careless handling on the way
to the printer. A photograph suffers considerable handling and
abuse before it ends up in print. Here are some pointers to help
prevent any deterioration of quality:

1. Keep surfaces clean.

2. Avoid using paperclips, writing in pen or lead pencil
   on the back of photos. Don't bear down too hard on overlays,
   or otherwise crack the emulsion and ruin the print.

3. Keep picture flat and use stiffeners.

4. Hold retouching to a bare minimum, and then have it done professionally.

5. Mark cropping instructions clearly.

6. Carefully guard both negatives and your last print. File by processing or negative number, subject, issue or article in a system that permits easy reference and quick reproduction of new prints from the old negative.

Fitting Photos to Your Page

Your printer can help "scale" photos in order to fit them attractively onto the page. You may want to let them run a full page apiece in some cases, and in others, group them for comparison and contrast. Whether the printer does the actual scaling or not, it will be helpful for you to understand the method used.

To begin, you should realize that it is not necessary to use (reproduce) the entire image area of any photo you might choose to include in your book. Say you have a photo of a garden with a person standing at the right edge. If you do not want that person to reproduce in your book, simply lay a ruler vertically along the right edge of the photo, and draw a line with a china marker from the top to bottom of the photo, excluding the person and all above and below him. This will give you a thinner photo obviously than you otherwise would have had. To get it back to the original proportion, you would have to chop some off the top or bottom. This exercise is called "cropping", and must be done prior to scaling.

Scaling is the reduction or enlargement of a photo or piece of art keeping it in proportion to its original size. In order to determine new dimensions of a photo you wish to reduce in order to fit into your book, a simple method is called the common diagonal.

See Sample I. You can start with a photo of any size. Let's say you want to reduce it to 4 inches wide. The question becomes, how tall will the new rectangle be?

To find out, lay a piece of tissue tracing paper over the photo and draw the diagonal A-C. It is handiest to draw the diagonal from lower left to upper right. Along A-B measure the new width, which is 4 inches (A-E). From E raise a perpendicular until it hits the diagonal at F. The distance E-F is then the height of the reduced rectangle.

The same method can be used to find the unknown width if instead you know only the height of the reduction you want. See Sample II. Now let's say you want to reduce this photo to a rectangle 5 inches tall. How wide is it going to be?

Once again, draw your diagonal X-T. Along X-U measure off the known new height, 5 inches, X-V. From V raise a perpendicular

It is not necessary to use the entire image area of any print you might wish to include in the book. If you wanted to reproduce only the hayrake in this beach scene, you would simply lay a straight edge ruler along the area you wish to keep and draw tic marks at the borders of the print. Keep the ruler parallel to the edges of the print. For purposes of illustration I marked on the image area of the

Sample I

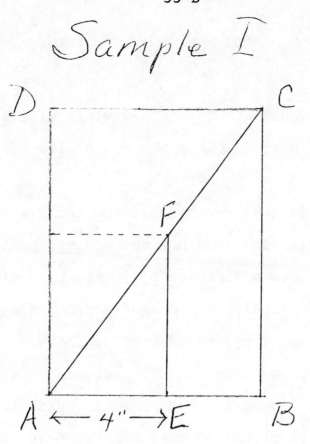

Sample II

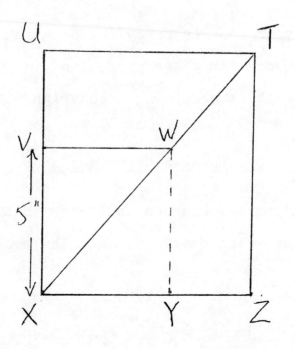

until it hits the diagonal at W. The new width will be V-W.
Then drawing the line W-Y, you have the exact size of the reduced
picture, X-Y-W-V.

The common diagonal method has the added advantage of
allowing you to mentally envision how the reduced photo will look.
If, for example, you have a photo of a flower, by noting its
relationship to the diagonal, you can get a good idea whether or
not it will be too small for good identification when reduced. If
so, the answer would be to crop out all extraneous matter in the
photo, then draw your diagonal. But remember, draw the diagonal
only on the part of the photo you wish to reproduce, and do not
include the areas you have cropped out.

PRE-PUBLICATION ACTIVITIES

Even before your book is ready for printing you can
begin to lay the groundwork for sales promotion. An early technical
point you can proceed with is obtaining a copyright.

Obtaining a Copyright

Copyrighting your book protects it from being reproduced
in any form without your written permission. The book must actually

be printed before you can file for copyright. Until publication
your book is protected by common law, but this becomes difficult
to prove in court should someone pirate your material. The best
defense in this case is the proverbial good offense. If you have
information that could easily be lifted by someone else and rushed
into production before your efforts see print, guard it carefully,
and, if necessary, create a simple contract agreement to protect
your information while working with suppliers.

When setting up the final drafts for your work, the
title page or backside of it must contain the copyright registration.
The notice must include three elements; name of the copyright owner,
year of publication and the word copyright, or its abbreviation (©).

SAMPLE: © Copyright 1975 by John Smith
Prior to the printing of your book you will want to write to the
Registrar of Copyright, Copyright Office, Library of Congress,
Washington, D.C. 20540. You will need the form called "Application
for Registration of a Claim to Copyright." Indicate that the book
will be published in the United States if that is the case.

You will receive a two page form containing questions
such as author, printer, their names and addresses, date of
publication and similar items.

When you have filled out the forms in duplicate, sign
them in front of a notary public. Send both copies of the completed

form along with two copies of your book and a $6 filing fee to the copyright office. Uncle Sam gives you a well deserved break by allowing you to mail the books postage free. Take them to the post office and make your request with the postmaster.

You will get one copy of the form back bearing the seal of the copyright office. Keep it in a fireproof box with the original copy of your manuscript as evidence of registration.

If you feel you want additional information on copyright procedures, or you have what you think is an unusual case, contact the copyright office and request a copy of Circular 35, entitled, "General Information on Copyright."

Obtaining Free Listings of Your Book's Title
Library of Congress Number

You can have your book listed free in the National Union Catalog which is used by libraries around the world to obtain books for their shelves. This simple matter of registration gives you exposure to thousands of potential buyers without any cost.

To obtain this Library of Congress Catalog Number write to the Chief of the Card Division, Library of Congress, Navy Yard Annex, Building 159, Washington, D.C. 20541. You must include the following information: Author's name, title, edition, date of publication, publisher's name and address, printer's name and address, if a series which segment will be copyrighted, approximate number of pages, and type of binding.

You must apply for this listing prior to printing your book since you will be assigned a number which must be printed on the reverse side of the title page as follows: Library of Congress Catalog Number _____.

Other Free Listings

You can also get your book listed free of charge in several indexes published by the R. R. Bowker Company, 1180 Avenue of the Americas, New York, New York, 10036. These include Books in Print, Publisher's Weekly and Paperback Books in Print. Libraries, bookstores, large discount stores and others use these lists as sources for purchases.

Also write to R. R. Bowker for forms necessary in obtaining an ISBN number which should also be printed on the reverse side of the title page. Many libraries and bookstores use this number for ordering, inventories and publisher identification.

You will also want to make sure your book finds its way after publication to the H. W. Wilson Company, 950 University

Avenue, New York, New York 10052, for free representation in the
Cumulative Book Listing. It is a catalog used by bookstores and
libraries for making purchases.

Publishing and the Law

As a self publisher it would serve you well to know some
of the thorny areas you can get into by putting words into print.
These pointers aren't intended as a substitute for legal counsel,
but rather will tip you off to potential trouble.

Broadly you should concern yourself with the rudiments
of copyright, right of privacy, libel and illegal reproduction.

Copyright pertains to words and the form in which they are
expressed. It does not extend to ideas. Common law copyright
places ownership of a letter with the sender rather than the
receiver. Thus you will want to get permission from the sender
of any letter you might want to use in testimonial advertising.

On the right of privacy the law is not really clear.
If a person does not wish to have his name mentioned in connection
with the advertising or promotion of a product (such as your book)
he has that right. However, if a person is a part of a news event,
even if a bystander at an accident, his picture and name can be
used without permission. If you obtain a written release you'll
never go wrong.

Libel is the derogatory mention of a person in your book, and this can be done in words or pictures. Check reprinted material for possible libel, since you can be charged even if you weren't the originator. Truth is a defense, but make sure your sources aren't rumors or fourth-hand accounts.

As for reproducing material that is illegal, just remember to avoid promoting lotteries, securities, money, financial schemes, stamps or activities that could be deemed obscene or fraudulent. Since your books will probably be sent through the U.S. mails, you will want to be particularly careful in these areas since a separate set of statutes applies for that purpose. Those laws do, however, cover basically the same general categories outlined above.

FORMING A BUSINESS

Perhaps the most important aspect of self publishing is the need to approach the merchandising of your book with the same attitude you would any other product. If you were to embark on the selling of automobiles, for example, you would not do so without a pre-designed format for conducting business. You need a system for keeping records, raising operating capital, contacting potential customers and the like. The need for a management structure is no less critical in merchandising your self published book to best sellerdom.

Approaching self publishing as a business venture offers several advantages. It forces you to think in terms of profit and loss at the early stages of producing your book. That fact will cause you to make decisions differently than you would if you were thinking of your manuscript as nothing more than an artistic entity. Also, creating a business structure forces you to keep records. This will be a structure you will be thankful for at income tax time since many business related expenses are deductible.

Finally, creating a business makes you examine your assets and liabilities as a self publisher. What do you have to offer? What are the strengths and weaknesses of your product? How can you develop your "game plan?"

Best Bet -- A Publishing Company

The most logical type of business for you to create is a publishing company. You will receive all the benefits of building your own business plus some others. For example, you might at some future date decide to publish the work of other authors. As you gain experience going through the steps of creating

a best seller of your own book, you might begin to see opportunities
to do the same with another author's work.

Another advantage for forming a publishing business is
the satisfaction that comes from making your influence felt on
our culture. As a creator and purveyor of the written word, you
will enjoy prestige and status unknown to rank and file citizens.
The title of publisher carries with it a degree of dignity, and
that fact alone might not hurt your ability to obtain capital either.

Start Your Own Advertising Agency

While discussing the formation of your business venture,
I would like to point out that I formed my own advertising agency
when I learned that the agencies received 15 percent of the bill
each time they placed ads for me.

You as a writer, are in an excellent position to be your
best copywriter, and will probably work harder than an agency you
could hire to promote your book. You will also be more alert to
specials and "deals" which provide you many opportunities to buy
ads at the lowest costs.

To start your own agency simply dream up a name for it
that is different from the name of your publishing company, and
get some stationery printed. (You also may wish to incorporate.

More on that later.) That much effort will entitle you to a 15
percent discount from most newspapers and magazines you will want
to advertise in.

If your interests do not lie along the lines of plugging
your book through advertising, it might be worth it to you to pay
an agency the 15 percent plus a small retainer customary with
smaller accounts. For that fee they will prepare ads, place them,
handle all billing, and do some testing to determine the effectiveness of various ads. While some of the larger and more diversified
agencies would not be interested in an individual account for a
single book, smaller ones are, particularly those who specialize
in promotion of self published books; such as Peterson Advertising
Agency, Inc., Suite 218, Beneficial Building, Wilmington, Delaware,
19801.

What Form for Your Business?

There are fundamentally three forms your business can
take: Proprietorship, Partnership and a Corporation. Each has
advantages and disadvantages which you can weigh in terms of your
own self publishing goals. Many individuals have been deterred
from incorporating because of the initial costs and the fact they
simply did not know how to go about it. For those reasons I
published my book, "How to Form Your Own Corporation Without a

Lawyer for Under $50." It contains tear out forms for everything you need including minutes, bylaws and the actual certificate of incorporation.

Here are some excerpts from that book outlining the advantages and disadvantages of each form of business.

"Advantages of Partnerships and Proprietorships

1. Somewhat lower cost to organize since there are no incorporating fees.

2. Less formality in record keeping.

3. The owners file one tax return.

4. Owners can deduct losses that might be incurred during the early life of a business from other personal income.

5. Pending legislation, if adopted, may increase the limit of tax deductible contributions to "Keogh" type pension and profit sharing plans which would reduce the tax advantage now available to a corporation.

6. Profits of a partnership, unlike dividends paid by a corporation are not subject to a second Federal income tax when distributed to the owners. However, whether this is an advantage, taxwise, depends on certain other factors namely:

a. The individual tax brackets of the owners as compared with that of the corporation.

b. The extent to which double taxation of earnings of the corporation is eliminated by deductible salaries paid to owners and by retention of earnings in surplus.

Disadvantages of Partnerships and Proprietorships

1. Unlimited personal liability. The owners are personally liable for all debts and judgments against the business, including liability in case of failure or other disaster.

2. In a partnership, each member can bind the other so that one partner can cause the other to be personally liable.

3. All profits are personally taxable to the owners at rates which may be higher than corporate rates.

4. There are not the tax advantages of benefit plans such as pension and profit sharing that are available to corporations. (The "Keogh" type plans for unincorporated businesses which do permit pension and profit sharing plans do not have the flexibility and tax shelters contained in corporate plans. There

is a limit or ceiling of $2,500 that any one
principal owner or partner can contribute toward a
profit sharing plan.)

5. If the owner(s) dies or becomes incapacitated, the
business often comes to a standstill.

6. The owner(s) does not have the full tax benefits of
the tax deductible plans including pension and profit
sharing that are available to a corporation.

Advantages of Incorporating

1. The personal liability* to the founders is limited
to the amount of money put into the corporation,
with the exception of unpaid taxes.

2. If a business owner wishes to raise capital, a
corporation is more attractive to investors who
can purchase shares of stock in it for purposes
of raising capital.

3. A corporation does not pay tax on monies it receives
in exchange for its stock.

4. There are many more tax options available to
corporations than to proprietorships or partnerships.
One can set up pension, profit sharing and stock

* As a publisher you may run added risks of libel for which you
would be held personally responsible.

option plans that are favorable to the owner of
the corporation.

5. A corporation can be continued more easily in the
event of the death of its owners or principals.

6. Shares of a corporation can easily be distributed
to family members.

7. The owners (stockholders) of a corporation that is
discontinued due to it being unsuccessful can have
all the advantages of being incorporated, yet be
able to deduct up to $25,000 on an individual tax
return or $50,000 on a joint return of money invested
in the corporation from personal income.

8. The owner(s), stockholders, of a corporation can
operate with all the advantages of a corporation,
yet be taxed on personal income tax rates if this
option provides a tax advantage.

9. Owners can quickly transfer their ownership interest
represented by shares of stock, without the
corporation dissolving.

10. The corporation's capital can be expanded by
issuing and selling additional shares of stock.

11. Shares of stock can be used for estate and family
planning.

12. The corporation can ease the tax burden of its stock-
    holders by accumulating its earnings. This is pro-
    viding the accumulation is not unreasonable and is
    for a business purpose.

13. It is a separate legal "being", separate and apart
    from its owner(s) (stockholders). It can sue and
    be sued and can enter into contracts.

14. A corporation may own shares in another corporation
    and receive dividends 85% of which are tax free
    subject to certain limitations.

Disadvantages of Incorporating

1. The owners of a corporation file two tax returns,
   individual and corporate. This may require added
   time and accounting expenses. (The owner of a proprietorship files one return; a member of a partnership files two.)

2. Unless the net taxable income of a business is
   substantial, i.e. $25,000 or more, there may not
   be tax advantages.

3. Maintaining the corporate records may require added
   time.

4. If debt financing is obtained by a corporation, i.e.
   a loan from a bank, the fund source may require the

personal guarantee by the owner(s) thereby eliminating the limited liability advantage of a corporation at least to the extent of the loan.

NOTE: Probably the biggest single disadvantage to incorporating prior to the publication of my book, was the high initial cost."

How to Raise Capital

As the owner of a valuable property (your manuscript) you have the primary ingredient necessary to attract capital. While you do not need a great deal of capital to enter self publishing, you will need some. And if you are willing to share some of the potential profits with others, you can approach the production and promotion of your book on an altogether different level than you would if it were a solo venture.

There are literally thousands of sources available for a businessman to raise operating capital, but few people know of any more than the local bank, a friend or perhaps a relative. For this reason I wrote and self published the book "Where the Money Is and How to Get It." The book contains over 2,000 sources of capital classified by name, address, telephone number and individual to contact.

Capital in a business can take the form of debt financing --
a loan, or equity financing -- (the sale of stock in a business).
Whichever form you decide is best for your business, the most
important factor in raising capital is the preparation of a carefully written plan. An outline of such a plan is included in the
book along with more than 2,000 sources.

Here are some areas of source capital that can help you
in your search. (Excerpts from "Where the Money Is and How to
Get It.")

"A. Loans through a bank, finance company, a factor
(who can use inventory as collateral), personal
friends, relatives, or private investors might loan
money to a new and promising company. The Small
Business Administration (SBA) is another source
to explore.

B. Private Offering - To avoid expense and time
involved with a Securities and Exchange Commission
(SEC) registration, shares of stock can be offered
in the corporation at a price per share that is
determined by the Director(s).

The number of people willing to pay the stock
price has to be limited. No more than 25 people can

be approached about investing in the corporation.

If more than 25 are approached, there may be violations of Federal and State SEC regulations regarding offerings of stock for which there are severe penalties.

These regulations hold that an offering to any more than 25 people is a 'public offering.' This type of offering must be registered.

C. Intra-State Offering - Shares of stock in the corporation may be offered to residents within the boundaries of any one state. There is no limit to either the number of persons approached or who become the stockholders. It may be wise to consult with an attorney and obtain the services of an accountant to prepare an 'Offering Circular' which describes the history, goals and purpose of the company and shows the financial status of it.

Investors should sign a 'subscription agreement' which states that the stock is being bought for investment and not for re-sale.

In all states, intra-state stock offerings must be registered with the State SEC.

D.   Public Offering - You can engage an underwriter who

will guide the corporation toward filing a prospectus

with the SEC for the purpose of selling shares in the

corporation to the public. 'Start-up', as well as

established companies can raise substantial funds by

selling a minority portion (less than 51%) of the

corporation. If the amount of capital sought is

$500,000 or less, the corporation may be able to

qualify under 'Regulation A', which is somewhat

shorter and a less costly procedure than a 'long

form' registration. When 'going public', it is

wise to consult with an attorney well versed in

SEC matters.

If one does form a Delaware corporation, the

state has competent attorneys knowledgeable in SEC

procedures due to the state's large corporation

activity. Over 72,000 corporations, including

two-thirds of all corporations on the American and

New York Stock Exchanges, are chartered there."

GETTING YOUR BOOK INTO PRINT

Choosing a Printer

Many printers are too large to consider a self published book. Their presses are designed to handle runs in the tens of thousands and up. This will be quickly evident in your early discussions with them. Avoid any attempts of a printer to persuade you to print a larger number of books than you feel you will be able to merchandise. Large printers make money on quantity, and they will explain how once the expensive cost of preparing type and plates is over, the cost of running extra copies comes down dramatically.

The cost per copy for a press run of 100,000 books might come to 50¢ while the cost per copy for 5,000 of the very same books might be $1.50. However, what you want to look at is the 95,000 books you probably won't be able to sell and the $50,000 TOTAL printing cost.

Instead, look for a smaller printer who will be willing to print fewer than 5,000 copies of your book. Many specialize in short runs and will be able to print a few hundred (See Section on Sources). While he probably will not have photo offset plate-making facilities on his premises, he will surely have a working relationship with a platemaker nearby who can provide quality service at a reasonable price.

As previously discussed, photo offset will generally produce better quality at a lower price than letterpress. And if you type the copy yourself in camera ready fashion, you should look to a price of roughly $1.00 per book for a quantity of 1,000.

Selecting Type and Style

If you want more variety than the IBM electric typewriter offers, or if for some reason you do not want to prepare the camera ready copy yourself, I would suggest using type set by photo composition, or "cold type." This will increase your costs somewhat, but you will have an almost infinite variety of type faces from which to select. The type will be set by a "type house" who works with your printer, and you will receive galley proofs to read and correct.

Here are some guidelines to help in selecting typefaces that will be best suited to your material. When purchasing typesetting you must specify type size and style, column width, and whether or not copy is to be justified (both margins even on each side of the column). The following information will help you in making those decisions most easily.

The specific goals of good typography are: select type-faces which are legible; arrange type in a manner which is inviting and readable; reduce reader fatigue; present what is written in an attractive manner; use type and designs which have appropriate connotations to the message.

Here is a summary of research findings on typography according to J. F. Sissors, Professor, Medill School of Journalism, Northwestern University.

Type faces in common use are about equally legible. Therefore, Caslon, Bodoni, Baskerville, Century, Times Roman, Goudy and Garamond, to name a few, are equally acceptable.

However, in a study of 10 type faces, Garamond was shown to be read 4% faster than any of the others. (Included in the test were: Scotch Roman, Antique, Bodoni, Old Style, Caslon Oldstyle, Kabel Light, Cheltenham Light, American Typewriter and Cloister Black.)

While small amounts of San Serif (characters have uniform thickness for example) type faces do not retard reading speed, large amounts may seriously affect reading speed and eye fatigue. When many pages of San Serif are used in a publication, the effect tends to be boring because of the similarity of letter shapes. In such cases, a type face having serifs would be much better.

Italic type faces, too, are read almost as fast as roman types when only a small amount of them appear on a page. Readers do not prefer large quantities of italic type faces, however, because they fear eyestrain. Therefore, italics should be used sparingly for body type. Best use of italics would be for contrasting headline, emphasis within a paragraph and citation.

Reading matter set in all capital letters is read about 12% slower than that set in caps and lower case.

While small amounts of bold face type are read almost as fast as light face, readers do not prefer bold face. They fear that it is more illegible than light face.

Three factors other than type style affect legibility. They are (a) the size of type; (b) the width of the line (measured in picas, 6 to an inch); (c) leading, the vertical distance from one line to the next. All three factors should be considered when planning the appearance of the printed page.

With Roman faces you will require less leading than with Sans Serif. So using a 10 point size and a line length of between 13 and 22 picas, two points of lead would be considered minimum and four points maximum.

Sample of Headline Type Faces

Arthur
VOL 2

aurora snug
VOL 1

Avalon® Ajar
VOL 8

Avalon® Light
VOL 8

Avalon® Medium
VOL 8

Avalon® Bold
VOL 8

Avalon® Shadowed
VOL 8

Baskerville Hound
VOL 1

Borealis
VOL 3

Bulletin
VOL 4

Celebration
VOL 5

Cheltenham X23
VOL 1

Corporate
VOL 4

CORP Image
VOL 4

Cranston
VOL 1

Crisis
VOL 3

Didoni
VOL 1

New Didoni
VOL 7

DImensia LIght
VOL 5

DImensia
VOL 2

Dominance
VOL 4

Dominance Bold
VOL 5

Dominance Diffident
VOL 4

Dominance Overbearing
VOL 4

Egyptian Surrounded
VOL 3

Eightball
VOL 6

Cueball: (EIGHTBALL OUTLINE)
VOL 6

Highball (EIGHTBALL SHADED)
VOL 6

Endowed Jones
VOL 2

Fat Chance
VOL 4

Ghost of a Chance
VOL 4

Fotura BIFORM Light
VOL 5

Fotura BIFORM Med
VOL 5

Fotura BIFORM Demi
VOL 7

Fotura BIFORM Open
VOL 7

Fotura Ultra Black
VOL 1

Goudy Flair
VOL 1

HAREM
VOL 1

Sample of Text Type in Various Sizes

___

NEWS GOTHIC BOLD

6 point
How often do you stop short in the midst of talking or writing because you can't think of the right word? More often than you like to realize? It's emb arrassing—and very annoying. The idea is clear in your mind. The word w
abcdefghijklmnopqrstuvwxyz 1234567890$
ABCDEFGHIJKLMNOPQRSTUVWXYZ

7 point
How often do you stop short in the midst of talking or writing bec ause you can't think of the right word? More often than you like t o realize? It's embarrassing—and very annoying. The idea is clea
abcdefghijklmnopqrstuvwxyz 1234567890$
ABCDEFGHIJKLMNOPQRSTUVWXYZ

8 point
How often do you stop short in the midst of talking or writin g because you can't think of the right word? More often than you like to realize? It's embarrassing—and very annoying. T
abcdefghijklmnopqrstuvwxyz 1234567890$
ABCDEFGHIJKLMNOPQRSTUVWXYZ

9 point
How often do you stop short in the midst of talking or wri ting because you can't think of the right word? More ofte n than you like to realize? It's embarrassing—and very an
abcdefghijklmnopqrstuvwxyz 1234567890$
ABCDEFGHIJKLMNOPQRSTUVWXYZ

10 point
How often do you stop short in the midst of talking or writing because you can't think of the right word ? More often than you like to realize? It's embarras
abcdefghijklmnopqrstuvwxyz 1234567890$
ABCDEFGHIJKLMNOPQRSTUVWXYZ

11 point
How often do you stop short in the midst of tal king or writing because you can't think of the r ight word? More often than you like to realize?
abcdefghijklmnopqrstuvwxyz 1234567890$
ABCDEFGHIJKLMNOPQRSTUVWXYZ

12 point
How often do you stop short in the midst o f talking or writing because you can't think of the right word? More often than you like
abcdefghijklmnopqrstuvw 1234567890$
ABCDEFGHIJKLMNOPQRSTUVWXYZ

14 point
How often do you stop short in the mi dst of talking or writing because you c an't think of the right word? More ofte
abcdefghijklmnopqrst 1234567890$
ABCDEFGHIJKLMNOPQRSTUVWXY

16 point
How often do you stop short in th e midst of talking or writing becau se you can't think of the right wor
abcdefghijklmnopq 1234567890$
ABCDEFGHIJKLMNOPQRSTUV

18 point
How often do you stop short i n the midst of talking or writi ng because you can't think of
abcdefghijklm 1234567890$
ABCDEFGHIJKLMNOPQRST

PICAS:	10	12	14	16	18	20	22	24	26	28	30
6 pt.	35	42	49	56	63	70	77	84	91	98	105
7 pt.	31	37	43	49	56	62	68	74	80	87	93
8 pt.	28	33	39	44	50	56	61	67	72	78	84
9 pt.	26	31	37	42	47	53	58	63	69	74	80
10 pt.	24	29	34	39	43	48	53	58	63	68	73
11 pt.	22	26	31	35	40	44	49	53	58	62	67
12 pt.	20	24	29	33	37	41	45	49	53	58	62
14 pt.	17	21	24	28	31	35	38	42	45	49	52
16 pt.	15	18	21	24	26	31	34	37	40	43	46
18 pt.	13	15	18	21	23	26	29	31	34	37	40
18E pt.	14	16	19	22	25	28	30	33	35	39	44

Avoid Author's Alterations

In purchasing typesetting you will have to pay a fee over and above whatever the basic typesetting charge quoted for any changes you make to your original manuscript. If changes become significant, they can cost more than the original quote. So do all your writing and rewriting at the manuscript stage, not on galley proofs.

Working with Your Printer

When working with a printer it is important to communicate your ideas briefly and accurately. If you use the following symbols to mark all copy and corrections, you will reduce the possibility of error due to a lack of common understanding. These markings are fairly universal among writers, publishers and printers. They are adapted from symbols used by Associated Press International Wire Service.

Copy Markings

Marking	Instruction
¶ATLANTA -- When organization of	paragraph
ᴖ is over. ⌐Now it will be the first	paragraph

Marking	Instruction

the last attempts.)

    With this the conquering is to — no paragraph

according to ~~the~~ this compendi- — delete

the Jones\Smith/firm is not in the — transpose

over a period of sixty or more in — use figures

there were 9 in the party at the — spell

Ada, Oklahoma, is in the lead at — abbreviate

the Ga. man is to be among the — spell out

prince edward said it is his to — capitals

accordingly This will be done — lower case

the acc user pointed to them — join

in|these times it is necessary to — separate

the order for the ~~later~~ devices — retain

BF/ or BF] By DONALD AMES [— bold (black) face centered

        J.R. Thomas] — flush right

[A.B. Jones Co. — flush left

president in a fine situation — insert

\# space

quotation marks, apostrophe

comma

period

= hyphen

⊢⊣ dash

a̱ u̱ n t (underline a u)

d ō n̄ e (overline o n)

Proofreader's Symbols

Symbol and Example	Instruction
# It is all right	insert space
⌒ It is al ways	close up
(:) instructions one, the	insert colon
⌀ time frammes	delete
⊙ So goodbye,	insert period
◡ Today, after I go,	insert comma
◠ two the first is	insert semicolon
?/ Says who	insert question mark
!/ Says me	insert exclamation mark
⌣/⌣ she's fine	enclose in quote marks
|=| a half baked nut	insert hyphen
|—| dollar now if you	insert dash
ital. and Nick Peterson said	reset in italics
Sm. cap. try Adolph's Formula	reset in small caps
caps come to canada	reset in caps
bf. Cliff McGoon announced	reset in bold face

tr. try a/one new) transpose

stet ~~said~~ Mr. Smith let stand

sp Market (St). spell out

‖ ‖ (Baynard Blvd. is align

L Baynard Blvd. is bring to mark

¶ Baynard Blvd. is new paragraph

no ¶ Baynard ~~Blvd~~ Blvd. is no paragraph, run together

Watch for the Following Problems

The things you will want to watch for when the printer begins the actual running of your job are bad register, poor ink quality, poorly made plates, or bad paper stocks. Each of these can turn good design, tasteful typesetting and perfect copy preparation into a finished monstrosity.

The most important factor for you to remember is to communicate to your printer just the degree of quality you expect to see in his finished work. You can help bridge the communications gap by examining his samples when you are initially shopping for a printer. Show him what you want done, see samples of his work, and get a price quote, not an estimate. Make your final decision on price, quality, and reputation, if possible.

When looking at printing samples, if they are grey looking and washed out, then you can judge the presswork was not good. If you detect pinholes, "doughnuts" and black specks on the finished copy, the plates were carelessly made. Beware of a printer who shows you samples with these or other apparent defects.

Printers often have excuses (they call them reasons) for work that doesn't meet customer needs. To be certain you get what you want and expect make sure your printer knows your requirements; then stay on top of him to convince him you care.

18 Ways to Reduce Your Printing Costs

1. Work with your printer and seek his advice on cost saving procedures.

2. Consult early with all your suppliers to avoid wasted time, motion and materials.

3. Make up a schedule with realistic deadlines for everyone concerned. If you miss a deadline, you cannot really expect your printer to make the time up on his end.

4. Avoid rush jobs, last minute changes and overtime charges.

5. Keep a list of printing charges such as overtime, author's alterations, over-runs, paperstock costs and "extras."

6. Get your printer to agree to submitting detailed bills with the major cost areas listed. Check charges against original bids periodically.

7. If you have type set, cut it BEFORE sending it to be set. It might be costing you a dime for every word you later delete.

8. Double check all statistics, names, places and facts.

9. Submit all copy flat, not rolled.

10. When correcting galleys, count characters to make a new line the same length as the one it replaces when making a change.

11. If you miss a mistake on the manuscript, it will cost you more to catch it on the galley, and more yet on the page proof. So read carefully, early.

12. Avoid resetting type once it has been set. If copy is too long in galleys, cut whole paragraphs. If too short, add sub heads, assuming you have them throughout.

13. Be careful with artwork. Keep it covered in transit and storage.

14. Deliver your whole job complete -- copy, photos, artwork. Also return corrected galleys with pasteups (on offset jobs.)

15. When choosing paperstock, ask your printer if the length of your press run will affect the price. He might have a sheet he will sell cheap but lacks enough to do your entire quantity. Do you need that many?

16. Make sure you select an appropriate paper sheet for your job. No need to pay the high cost of a quality sheet if it is not needed. Many mills have dropped cheap sheets, so you have to shop. Do so.

17. If you want to see press proofs, check them at the printing plant. Otherwise you're charged press time while your job is being delivered and approved.

18. Keep a source record for all material you might be called upon later to identify.

Now that You are Published

I am willing to bet that the world's greatest book was either never published at all, or else it never sold out of its first printing.

As a publisher I am intimately aware of the "unmined gold" that I know is lying around in the form of unpublished manuscripts and poorly promoted books. That's why an author's old works are dredged up and given cosmetic changes when he connects with a

winner. Suddenly all the manuscripts that were rejected, and all

his books which died because of low key promotion, are hot

properties.

The feature that makes this book unique is my formula

for creating a "bestseller." The key word there is SELLER. What

you want to do now is connect with that one book and let your future

successes flow naturally from that.

With the information I have discussed so far in the

book, you have the knowledge to get your manuscript into print at

the least cost and with maximum effectiveness. That in itself

will separate you from the gloomy side of the next batch of

statistics -- or how to join the elite ranks of those 400 authors

whose books sell out of their first printing.

Here's where I can really help.

YOUR SELLING GAME PLAN

Now that you've a.) chosen a bestselling subject and

tested it, and b.) gone through the necessary steps to get your

manuscript into print, and c.) found sources for raising capital,

you are ready to d.) develop a merchandising "game plan."

I have found that the best method of merchandising a book to bestseller status is through direct mail selling. It is the best way to reach large numbers of potential buyers at the lowest cost. Inherent in the success of a direct mail business is effective advertising, and I'd like to spend some time on that subject now.

While Madison Avenue moguls have built the image of advertising into frighteningly complex proportions, it really need not be. There are some basic pointers you will need in order to get your message across to the specific buying public you seek, and those pointers I'll help provide.

The media you might want to use in order to reach the book buying public include TV (talk show and spot commercials), radio, newspapers, magazines and trade journals (books for specific professions, such as horticulturalists).

Over the course of a year or more you should expect to spend a sizable sum of money on advertising and promotion if you are intent on building your book to bestseller status. However, the money will not need to be put up as advance capital, but rather should flow from pyramiding revenue derived from sales. For example, if you purchase a classified ad for $20 and realize $40 in sales, you net $20 profit on the transaction. Part of the $20 then goes

into more advertising to generate more sales, and so on. The
secret lies in spending advertising dollars only where they generate
sales. In that regard, there is no such thing as an expensive or
a cheap advertising medium. They are only expensive or cheap
relative to the sales dollars they pull in for you. That is, if
a full page in "PLAYBOY" costs $30,000, but you receive sales of
$60,000 as a result, "PLAYBOY" was not too expensive for you, and
you made a shrewd advertising buy. On the other hand, if you spend
$20 for a third of a page in the "PODUNK DAILY BLATT" and you
receive zero in sales, you have wasted $20. The measure of success
is profit. Some direct advertisers use the rule of thumb "income
must at least double the cost of the advertising."

How to Get the Best Advertising Buys

You always have the option of finding an advertising
agency to help with the problem of getting your message out.
Thousands of small agencies exist by employing the same techniques
I'll be going into shortly. Whether you choose to employ an agency
for part of your promotion effort or not, it will be worthwhile
for you to think through the steps involved in preparing an ad for
your book.

Preparing Your Ad

It is not an oversimplification to say that nearly every ad, regardless of its degree of sophistication, follows the Attention-Interest-Desire-Action formula. Particularly direct mail ads.

The first step in ad preparation is to sit down and think of every possible thing about your book that anyone could find of value in it. You ought to come up with 20 points or so. Things like choosing a garden site, correct size, drainage, how to test soil, proper rotation of vegetables and fruits, most effect/least expensive fertilizer and so on.

This exercise will point up features of the book which will result in selling points in the ad.

Then begin to fashion a headline. It should be attention getting and be set in bold face type. Frequently it is the title of the book, or perhaps one of the titles that you experimented with in the title testing phase. Seek provocative words. "Myths of Organic Gardening Exploded." Avoid hyperbole and superlatives such as revolutionary, fantastic. They have been overused to the point of having no meaning.

The next element is the subhead, or first paragraph. This should explain or amplify the headline, and is analogous to the first page in a book. Sample: "This exciting new book describes in detail all one needs to know about organic gardening."

The next step is the Introduction of the Features. This important line should read something like: "Here are some of the highlights revealed."

Next are the Features themselves. Select at least three or four. Include as many as space permits.

The next element amounts to what people are saying about the book. "Really helped me grow a better garden last year." In your first ads you can leave this section out until you have suitable testimonials.

You should include a drawing or photo of the book.

Then you want to have some background information on the author. You might want to include a photo of yourself here since surveys have shown photographs of people in an ad assure greater readership.

A crucial point is the GUARANTEE. Stress that you offer a full refund if not satisfied.

Finally, your ad should contain a coupon. Make sure it is reproduced large enough so name and address, etc. can be easily filled in.

As advertised in the Wall Street Journal, Barrons, National Observer, New York Times, Fortune, Business Week, Nations Business , etc.

How to form your own corporation without a lawyer for under $50.⁰⁰

By Ted Nicholas

HOW TO FORM YOUR OWN CORPORATION WITHOUT A LAWYER FOR UNDER $50.00 by Ted Nicholas

You may have considered incorporating. I'm sure you want to accomplish this in the most economical way. You may already be in business and are looking for ways to save tax dollars or limit personal liability.

You can benefit from this report if you are planning a one man business if you are associated with a partner or are the owner of a large company.

This exciting report shows you step by step how you can accomplish this for less than $50.00.

It contains tear-out forms for everything that is needed! This includes minutes, bylaws, and the actual certificate of incorporation!

It is presented in simple, clear language.

You'll learn of the many benefits of incorporating either an existing business or one that is planned.

Some of the features of the 8½ x 11, 30,000 word, 103 page report:

How you can incorporate without any capital requirement with zero capital.

The many personal tax benefits of incorporating.

How a corporation limits the personal liability for the owner(s) of a business, to the investment in the corporation. (Except for taxes)

How to actually form a corporation step by step. Included are instructions on completing the forms.

How to own and operate a corporation anonymously if desired. This assures maximum privacy.

How to form a non profit corporation. How to utilize tax "gimmicks" to personal advantage.

Find out why lawyers charge huge fees for incorporating services even when often times they prefer not to.

Learn how and why you can legally incorporate without the services of a lawyer. There is a fallacy in that most people feel it is necessary to have a lawyer to incorporate.

How to form an "open" or "close" corporation and the difference between them. Report contains tear out forms.

Sub Chapter S Corporations. What they are. How to set one up. How to operate a business as a corporation, yet be taxed on individual tax rates if more advantageous.

Learn about the many dangers and hazards of not incorporating partnerships and proprietorships.

What a Registered Agent is. How assistance is provided to individuals who incorporate. The most economical company to use. A complete section on this.

How to cut out all fees of the "middle man" normally involved in forming a corporation.

How a *"professional"* can benefit from incorporating.

How to save from $300 to over $1,000 in the formation of the corporation alone!

What a *"foreign"* **corporation is.** A State by State list of the filing fees involved in registering a "foreign" corporation.

Learn how a corporation can sell its stock to raise capital at any time.

How a single individual can be President, Secretary and Treasurer. There is no need to have anyone involved except a single stockholder although, of course, as many as desired can be included.

How to arrange for any stock sold to an investor in a corporation to be tax deductible to the investor's personal income in the event of loss. This makes the sale of stock in a corporation far more attractive to an investor.

An outline of the many situations where an individual would benefit by incorporating

How to legally incorporate and sell stock in a corporation without "registering" the stock.

What par and no-par value stock is and which is the most practical.

How an existing, unincorporated business anywhere in the United States can benefit by incorporating. Also included are the steps to take after incorporating.

The reasons why ⅔rds of the corporations listed on the American and New York Stock Exchanges incorporate in Delaware—the State most friendly to corporations—and how you can have the same benefits as the largest corporations in America.

What to do if you are already incorporated in another state and want to take advantage of incorporating in Delaware, without ever visiting the State.

Learn why many "side" businesses and investments should be separately incorporated.

Just complete the coupon below and your report will be promptly mailed to you.

IRON CLAD GUARANTEE. If you are not completely satisfied with the book after you have it for 10 days you may return it for a full refund.

COMMENTS FROM READERS
"I want to buy several copies for my clients."—Insurance Executive
"If I'd known about this I would have incorporated years ago."—Salesman
"This report is a handy reference for me."—Lawyer
"The author is experienced in the corporate world, giving him the qualifications to write this book."—Judge
"Fantastic! Do you want a partner?"—Lawyer
"Good idea. Brings the concept of being incorporated within the reach of anyone."—Artist
"I was quoted a price of $1,000 each for 3 corporations I want to form! This report saves me almost $3,000!"—Business Owner
"Excellent! Written so that anyone can understand it."—Secretary
"Takes the mystery out of forming a corporation."—Printer
"Very well written. Will encourage many small businesses to incorporate."
—Housewife
"Well written. Will eventually produce more business for lawyers."—Lawyer
"Great idea! I'd be glad to promote it for a piece of the action."
—Advertising Executive
"Should be in every business library."—Executive
"Will be forming two new corporations in January using this method."
—Publisher

Mr. Nicholas has been to the White House to personally meet with the President of the United States after being selected as one of the outstanding businessmen in the Nation. © Copyright Enterprise Publishing Co. 1975

Suggested Advertising Copy — Full page Magazine size 7" x 10"

INSTRUCTIONS

These ads are "camera ready". Use these fully tested ads in your publication, newspaper, magazine, and trade journal, etc. merely cut out desired ad.

Once the ad is written you can compare it to other mail order ads for size and number of words. In this manner you can estimate how many words you can use for different size ads. In general, mail order ads are more wordy than an ad for, say, toothpaste.

Even if you go to an advertising agency, you will have to go through the same basic exercise as just discussed. What the agency experts will do is help you put your ideas and knowledge into the correct form.

Once you have the material written, you will have to find a graphic designer to help arrange the ad on a page attractively, and to have reproduction proofs made. Find one who moonlights either at an advertising agency or on a medium to large circulation newspaper. He will help you get the ad set in type. Typical cost should be about $75 to $200.

How to get Free Advertising and Publicity

Even free advertising is wasted if it fails to generate sales. However, it is rare that advertising fails to stimulate at least some degree of customer curiosity, assuming, of course, the message is not entirely misplaced.

By itself free advertising will not provide enough promotional oomph to create a bestseller. However, it can be used in

conjunction with paid advertising to provide broader coverage. It
can also be used to test the effectiveness of a medium about which
you are in doubt since you can shift the risk.

A prime method of advertising at no cost is the "P.I."
deal. P.I. stands for per inquiry. This means the newspaper,
magazine, radio or TV station runs your ad without cost to you.
Then, when the orders come in, they take their cut (usually 33 - 50
percent) of the retail selling price and send the balance to you.
As you can see, you spread the risk and also the profit. For that
reason you would not want to enter into a P.I. deal with a medium
you have tested with good results. In that case, why split the
profits? Instead, pay for your advertising and collect all the
revenue.

How to Approach the Media -- The "Pitch Letter"

The best way to approach busy TV and radio talk show
hosts is through a short, personal letter stating two or three of
the most interesting aspects of your material and about yourself.
Such a letter ought to be written, or at least signed by someone
other than yourself. TV people particularly are used to dealing
with a third party, and also this eliminates any implication of
boastfulness.

In picking two or three points to mention about your book, you can draw upon the same ones you used in making up the circular discussed in the section on Title Testing. Or, you can approach the problem anew either by yourself, or with the help of an advertising agency in the form of an exploratory meeting. Even a friend can help if you ask him to sum up the contents of your book in one or two paragraphs.

To capture the TV host's attention, it is best if you wrap your nuggets of information around some topical problem of the day, such as, "Mr. Smith's book, 'Secrets of Organic Gardening' helps provide answers to today's shrinking food dollar." Then go on in the letter to reveal a few of your secrets.

The important thing to remember is that these people on TV and radio are constantly looking for fresh, new material to present to their viewers or listeners. Most appear five days a week, and even a 5 or 10 minute show runs through a lot of material in a month's time. They look for authors as a prime material source, and it is also in your favor to be local. However, don't let that deter you from contacting stations away from your immediate locale. Be sure to include any personal accomplishments or activities that the interviewer might discuss with you on the air.

In your letter you will want to close with a request for

Sample of pitch letter to TV and Radio stations

Contact - Peterson Advertising Agency   Nov. 26 -- LAS VEGAS
          Suite 507, Beneficial Bldg.   27 -- LOS ANGELES
          Wilmington, Del. 19801   28 -- "   "
   Phone: (302) 656-8750   29 -- "   "
                                                     30 -- San Diego
                                              Dec. 1 -- "   "
                                                     3 -- SACRAMENTO
AVAILABLE for INTERVIEW   4 -- SAN FRANCISCO
                                                     5 -- "   "
     T E D   N I C H O L A S
          author of
          HOW TO FORM YOUR OWN CORPORATION WITHOUT A LAWYER FOR UNDER $50
                                        (Enterprise Publishing Co.)

ABOUT THE BOOK --

-- now in its 4th printing, it is geared for both the one-man businessman
   and for the owner of large companies--telling us all we will ever want
   to know about incorporating

-- the motivating factor behind this book is the author's strong belief
   in the concept that an individual businessman should have available
   to him the knowledge and benefits heretofore available only to the
   largest corporations in America

-- goes into advantages of incorporating, including tax and stock benefits,
   how to operate anonymously and the advantages of incorporating in the
   state of Delaware, the friendliest state in the Union to corporations

-- describes how businessmen can save countless amounts of money in legal
   fees--in clear layman terms--complete with tear-out forms, minutes,
   by-laws and everything else that is needed to properly incorporate

ABOUT THE AUTHOR --

-- now an enthusiastic 39 year old author-businessman, he has been in
   his own business since the age of 22

-- during the course of his business career, he has founded 18 corporations
   in diverse businesses, including food, confectionery, real estate,
   machinery and licensing--all were small businesses

-- has experienced success and failure and often states that he has
   learned more from failure than from success

-- having gained first-hand experience in the business world, he decided
   there was a need for a book on incorporating, directed toward the
   small businessman

                                                    (cont'd.)

Page #2

-- a few years ago he was selected as one of the nation's outstanding
   businessmen and was invited to meet with Pres. Lyndon Johnson
   at the White House

-- also maintains The Company Corporation, serving corporations of
   all sizes throughout the U.S. with corporate services

===

ENTERPRISE PUBLISHING CO.   1300 Market St.   Wilmington,Del. 19801

Sample of letter for Radio and TV Talk Shows

As the job market shrinks and prices skyrocket, more and more of your listeners are starting their own businesses. Many women now work out of their homes to supplement the family income. To keep up with increased money needs, others with hobbies are expanding them into businesses, while keeping a full time job.

Your audience has heard how all the big companies legally save fortunes through incorporation tax savings. It's totally legitimate, but infuriating! Although your listeners could take advantage of these same savings, most do not. Why? Because they think incorporating is too expensive. Lawyers' charges run as high as $1,000. -- too expensive for a home-run business. Very often that's the entire profit.

Ted Nicholas will tell your listeners that attorney's services are not required by law to incorporate. Mr. Nicholas says that incorporating any business should cost no more than $50.

More than 100,000 copies of Ted's book HOW TO FORM YOUR OWN CORPORATION WITHOUT A LAWYER FOR UNDER $50, have been sold for $7.95. Mr. Nicholas has been to the White House to meet with the President of the United States, after being selected as one of the Nation's outstanding businessmen.

Articulate, outspoken, and knowledgeable, Ted Nicholas is ready to discuss the advantages, as well as the costs, of incorporating. He can alert your listeners to businesses they can start with little or no capital.

In the Wall Street Journal and numerous national magazines, people have been reading about Ted Nicholas' book, published by Enterprise Publishing, a member of the Better Business Bureau of Delaware. We hope you'll agree that Mr. Nicholas will make an excellent guest for your show. Please let us know what dates are available on your show in the next two months. Meanwhile, please don't hesitate to call us if we can be of help.

Sincerely,

a specific day for your appearance. It helps to offer a framework
of a week or so for the host to work around. With the first
letter you can simply enclose the sales circular for your book.
When you get scheduled, the host will undoubtedly request a copy of
the book if it has been printed.

Through this method I have booked appearances on over 100
radio and TV shows throughout the U.S.

How to Promote Your Book Through Magazine Articles

An excellent means of obtaining free publicity is to offer
to write a magazine article about your subject. In order to engineer
such a deal, you should write to the editor of an appropriate
magazine mentioning that you will be willing to write an article
for his magazine at no cost to him. Say that you will slant it
toward the magazine's audience. Tell him that all you would like
in return is mention at the end saying you are the author and
where readers can buy your book.

You have two things working for you in such an arrangement. First, you as an author are an authority in your field, and
magazines want authorities writing articles for them. Second, most
publications are on tight budgets, and mention of a "freebie" makes

HOW TO ...
AVOID LOSSES AND GAIN BENEFITS AS A SMALL BUSINESSMAN

By TED NICHOLAS

SPECIALTY SALESMAN

SEPTEMBER, 1975

As an unincorporated small businessman you may be exposing yourself to unnecessary hazards. These can be avoided by incorporating. While helping thousands of individuals with small businesses, I have seen many problems that can be serious.

Unfavorable conditions that arise in the course of doing business are often beyond your direct control. An example of this was exhibited during the energy crisis.

Thousands of independent gasoline dealers had to close their businesses. They simply could not get enough product (gasoline) to sell to their customers. Too many of the unincorporated dealers lost everything they had. When they closed the business many were personally liable for all the business debts. Some of them were sued for these debts and lost their homes, savings, even their furniture.

You may be building a family business. If you were killed in an accident, your business would probably be liquidated even though it might be advantageous to keep it going for the benefit of the family. A corporation can be more easily continued.

If you were to buy a franchise by making a down payment and personally signing a promissory note, you would incur a large debt. With a promissory note signed by you personally, if the business does not succeed, as an unincorporated businessman you are liable.

If you are an importer and without your knowledge you inadvertently sell defective merchandise, and someone is injured because of it, you can be sued personally along with the manufacturer.

If things went badly in your business and you were forced into personal bankruptcy, you would not only lose your assets, you would lose your legal right to declare bankruptcy again for six years.

All of the foregoing problems and hazards can be avoided by setting up a corporation. You immediately protect yourself against them.

I've helped thousands of people form corporations at low cost. If you have a close friend who is a lawyer and who knows your personal assets and credit rating are in jeopardy because of your business, I am sure he would advise you to protect yourself through incorporating.

My book shows you how to set up a corporation at the lowest possible cost. If you retain a lawyer, by using the book you will save him time and yourself money.

You can now form a corporation by completing some simplified forms, which takes only a few moments. You create, with the stroke of a pen, a separate legal entity. This is as though a new person was born at a separate time from you. The corporation can enter contracts, sign leases and buy and sell property. You personally are protected if things do not go as planned.

When you require business capital you can borrow money or sell shares in the corporation. If you require large amounts of capital you can sell shares widely and "go public."

If you are sued or have any type of business disaster your personal assets are separate from those in your corporation. In the event something happens to you in an accident, the business can easily be continued or ownership transferred.

You can be a one-man corporation if you desire, without having to bring in outsiders. You can act as president, vice president, and secretary.

If your corporation experiences business setbacks and cannot meet its obligations on time, the business can be reorganized. In the event things go poorly and the business is forced into bankruptcy, you can form a new corporation immediately and obtain a fresh start. Your personal credit is not affected.

Through tax deductible benefit plans and other tax benefits, you as an individual with a small or even one-man corporation can obtain the same benefits as the largest corporations in America. If you haven't considered forming your own corporation, perhaps now is the time to do so. **SS**

Sample of Magazine Article

an editor's heart warm. When you contact the editor, tell him you have an outline of your article written. Make sure you have studied the magazine to see what type of articles it generally runs.

Magazines of all sizes and types run articles like this. I have had many of this nature published. It is an excellent means of gaining exposure for both yourself and your book.

Testimonials

Testimonials are an effective method of free promotion because people are interested in the comments and reactions of other people. Endorsement of a product by one person tends to lower the inherent sales resistance of another.

In order to turn this natural sales resistance to your advantage, you should develop "solicited" testimonials early in the lifecycle of your book. Perhaps while still in the manuscript stage you can show it to friends, neighbors, fellow workers, relatives and others to read and comment. If you use their names and remarks in subsequent advertising and promotion, you must have their permission, preferably in the form of a written release stating that they give you complete license to use their names and comments about your book in your advertising efforts. Most people won't mind, and will, in fact, be flattered.

In many cases it will not be convenient, or even possible, to obtain written permission. In such cases you can simply use the person's remarks and his initials, such as "J.T., chemist, Wilmington, Delaware."

By obtaining solicited testimonials early in the development of your promotional effort, you can incorporate them into your title testing circular, the book jacket (if hard cover), the cover itself (if paperback) and all advertising.

Still another way to obtain solicited testimonials is by inviting readers to participate in a testimonial contest. I have included a sample letter (See page #73-A) which was productive. You can use this for ideas in preparing your own if you wish.

As sales begin, you will start to receive unsolicited testimonials, and they can be used in the same fashion following the same rules for permission.

The Autograph Party

Still another little or no cost method of promoting your book is by conducting an autograph party at one or more bookstores. Many books, of course, lend themselves to this kind of personal touch promotion.

Sample of successful letter to obtain testimonials.

Dear Customer:

We invite you to join a fun contest! It will only take a few minutes of your time and you have a good chance to make some money!

We are seeking additional testimonials for the Ted Nicholas book WHERE THE MONEY IS AND HOW TO GET IT. Your name was picked at random from our list of buyers.

We are interested in obtaining comments from satisfied customers that may be used in our nationwide advertising.

First prize for the best written testimonial will be $50. However, any testimonial resulting from this contest which is chosen for future advertising and publicity will be awarded a prize of $10.

All you need do is submit to us a copy of this letter, using the bottom portion of this page, stating in 25 words or less the reasons you liked and/or benefited from this book.

We look forward to receiving your reply.

Sincerely,

TESTIMONIAL CONTEST ENTRY FORM
"I BENEFITED FROM THE BOOK 'WHERE THE MONEY IS AND HOW TO GET IT' IN THE FOLLOWING WAYS" . . . .

_____

_____

_____

It is my understanding that if I am the winner of this contest I will receive a check for $50. It is my further understanding that if my testimonial is to be used, that I will be paid $10. In either case, I hereby consent that my testimonial may be used. My name or initials (circle which you prefer) as well as the city and state in which I reside may be used in your advertising and publicity.

_____   _____
                                    Name

_____   _____
Signature   Street Address

                                    _____
                                    City   State   Zip

The procedure is quite simple. Start by contacting bookstores in your local area who would logically like to tie in with a local author. You can call or drop them a note indicating you will be available on certain days to be at the bookstore for an "autograph party." The book shop can promote this in the local newspaper and hopefully attract additional customers to the store to purchase a book signed by you, the author. Later, if and when you go on a regional or national tour of radio and TV shows, it is a good idea to tie in with book shops in the areas in which you appear for such autograph parties. You can contact these stores in advance of your appearances on these shows. For this purpose, it is often helpful to have a letter composed on your advertising agency stationery.

I have had experiences with autograph parties that range from very successful -- with people waiting in line to purchase a copy of the autographed book, to somewhat lonely events when just a few people would drop by. Oftentimes, even if a large volume of book sales does not materialize, local publicity beneficial to you (and the bookstore) can result.

In fact publicity of this type helps to make your mail order advertising more effective.

Newspaper Columnists and Book Reviewers

Reviews beget sales. Even bad reviews tend to arouse reader curiosity about your book. The rule here is: try to get your book reviewed in print by as many people as you can. The caveat: don't waste copies of the book sending to people unlikely to write a review. How do you determine who's who?

Divide columnists and reviewers into two groups: 1.) those likely to do a review, and 2.) those you're not sure about. Remember, reviewers are more stimulated by receiving the actual book than are TV talk show hosts. (TV people are really as interested in YOU as in your book.) You, as an expert in your own field, will have a pretty good idea of who to send the book to for likely review. For the second group, let me suggest you select names from the lists of reviewers provided in this section, and send a cover letter offering a review copy of the book if they would be interested in receiving it.

If there is a syndicated reviewer in your field, e.g. "Gardening with Gordon," send a copy of the book on the first shot, with a covering letter.

To determine other potential reviewers, consult "Literary Marketplace," "Ayers Periodical Directory," and "Bacon's Publicity

Checker" (this has all publications organized by industrial classification, e.g. agriculture. These reference volumes are available in your local library.

Don't overlook the value of a review in your local paper or radio station. In fact, in a smaller town, a story about a local author can be page one news.

Additional publicity mileage can be obtained by writing your own review and having it printed in newspaper facsimile style. These "clips" can then be mailed to other papers and are effective in generating more publicity.

A professional reviewer named Art Martin, 533 E. Kelso Road, Columbus, Ohio 43202, will handle all details for you for a cost of around $50.

P.I. on TV and Radio

In addition to appearing on talk shows, you can explore P.I. deals on both radio and TV. In both cases it is necessary that you pay the cost of preparing the advertisement. You can contact a local TV station or studio and ask them to prepare a videotape for you. If you have a theatrical flair, you can save yourself the $50 or so a professional announcer costs. Since your product is your own book, it is not so important to have a polished, actor-type to

Sample of First Approach Letter to make P.I. arrangements.

TO: Radio Station Manager

Dear Mr _____:

        I would like you to call me collect _____.
Why? Because I have something that is going to make both of
us a lot of money!!! What? Our publication by Ted Nicholas,
HOW TO FORM YOUR OWN CORPORATION WITHOUT A LAWYER FOR UNDER $50.

        This book is the hottest "How To" book to come down the
pike in fifty years!!! A reader can use the tear out forms,
incorporate, and save hundreds of dollars. A lot of idle
bragging, not in the least. This concept has been tested by
readers in the United States, Canada, Europe, and Mexico by both
amateurs and pros. It's a proven system. It works.

        We're so sure of the sales success of this book that
we're putting our money where our mouth is. We're offering
this book for only $8.40 postpaid. The buyer can keep the
book for ten days; if he is not completely satisfied, we'll refund
his money. Fair enough?

        What all this means to you is PROFIT, because you keep
$3.36 for every order you receive. Let me send you our pre-
recorded (90 sec.) commercial, and a sample book for you
to incorporate with. Call or write me right now, and let's both
start making a lot of money!!!

                        Sincerely,

Enc: brochure

advertise it on a TV spot. The authenticity of your personal touch can go a long way toward offsetting inexperience.

The cost of producing a one-minute spot will be in the neighborhood of $200, with an additional $25 for each duplicate tape. Rather than just sending a tape to a TV station, I send a cover letter and sales brochure describing the book I am offering. In the letter I ask if they do P.I. advertising, and if they would be interested in running mine. Since P.I. advertising represents something of a risk to a station, it will select the product most likely to draw responses. Thus a good track record makes acceptance easier.

The reason the media accept P.I. advertising is to fill space not sold or filled with editorial matter.

P.I. in Print Media

The P.I. method works basically the same with all media. Many newspapers and magazines do P.I. advertising, especially the smaller ones. You will have to furnish the ad, ideally prepared in the form of a "reproduction proof." This is a copy of the ad printed on heavyweight glossy paper which allows for sharp, clear reproduction.

The publication will run the ad at no cost, and collect
33-50% of the retail selling price before sending the balance to
you.

You can solicit this medium by mail and follow up with
a phone call. In addition you can get good leads on P.I. availabilities
through advertising space representatives as well as from the advertising department of the publications themselves.

Ad Testing

Once you have your ad prepared, you are ready to test it.
It is best to be in a magazine or newspaper with which you are
familiar. This is, of course, assuming you are aiming toward the
correct market of potential buyers for your book. Pick an established one with an established following in order to give you a
standard of comparison against other publications of similar
content. Select a publication that has an Audited Bureau of
Circulation (ABC) figure available. The ABC verifies that a publication's circulation is what it is claimed to be. Not that any
publications lie, but some space salesmen tend to use "readership"
rather than "circulation" as an indication of how many readers the
book or paper has. Readership is determined (by the publication)
to be the number of people who actually see the periodical. A

single household will probably receive only one copy of a paper, for example, but all family members might read it. The kicker here is the word "might". When you receive a verified ABC appraisal of "circulation" you know for certain at least that number of people pay to obtain the information. You can easily assume that more than that number will ultimately see it, but for test purposes you want only figures that you can test against other similar publications.

A final reminder in choosing the publication for your first test ad is: don't pick the one with the most expensive advertising rates.

Conducting the Test

Get your ad placed on a right hand page. Make sure your "insertion order" (which can be just a typed letter) specifies this or else don't run the ad. I have found the response rate to be substantially higher for ads I have run in the first five right hand pages, or in the first one third of a magazine, regardless of what the space representatives say to the contrary.

Place your ad in the magazine, and wait 30 days. Approximately 60% of responses will be in within 30 days of the time the publication reaches the readers' hands. And don't be fooled by cover dates on magazines. Find out when the publication is mailed, and how long it takes to reach the market area you are buying.

Due to the fact that most magazines work at least a month in advance, and that it takes a month for returns to come to you, you might instead want to test in newspapers. This is especially true if your book is of general interest. If it is a special interest subject, like business, you can select a special interest newspaper, like the "Wall Street Journal." A newspaper gives you a decidedly better turnaround time for evaluating results.

Placement in Newspapers

Again, you want your ad placed on the right hand page. In a newspaper you want it above the fold, not below. If your book is business oriented, put it in the business section. If on gardening, put it in the gardening section. The most well read page in any paper is likely to be the TV page. If your book is of general interest or business, you might want to run it on the classi- fied page. Not as a classified ad, but as a display ad on the classified page.

In the case of newspaper testing, you will receive 60% of your responses in the first week. On the bad side of newspaper testing, you get very little "pass-along" readership, and a paper is usually tossed out much sooner than a magazine.

How to Get the Best Deal in Buying Advertising

When you have decided in which publications you wish to advertise, go to the library and check "Standard Rate & Data Service." This contains a complete listing of all publications and their advertising rates. With those figures in hand, contact either a space representative or the publication itself and ask if they offer a "publishers" mail order rate. It has been my experience that approximately 50% do. Tell them that you are testing your ad. And remember to point out that if it is successful, you will be a repeat customer. Don't haggle with them. If they are firm, and say their rate card rate is the same for General Motors or Joe's Beanery, then simply decide the value of that publication on the basis of its cost and probable return.

The important thing is to _ask_ for a special rate. Most big companies don't. Their advertising is placed through ad agencies, and those agencies receive their payment by taking 15% of the cost of placing the ads. So, it is not in their best interest to bargain for space rates. It is, however, in your best interest.

Buying Remnant Space

As the name implies, remnants are parts left over from a larger part. In the case of advertising, remnants are what remain when a large company buys space in a national publication, but only uses one region. For example, a pesticide producer might buy a page in "Farming Magazine" to reach cotton growers in the South. He's only interested in that geographic area, and you can pick up the remainder of the United States for up to 80% off the rate card price. Tell everybody you do business with that you are interested in picking up remnants. Since they are bargains, they tend to be passed out to good customers or those who show a potential of becoming good customers.

I'll offer some final bits of advice in dealing with advertising people. First, it's good strategy not to buy space on the basis of the first phone call. Space sales people will work harder to seek out bargains for you if you make them work at it. The second point, in the same vein, become friendly with the space sales representative in your area. It can make the difference between his calling you with a bargain or his calling someone else.

Ask for Free Editorial Coverage

When you purchase advertising space from a publication, it is more or less customary with many to provide you with a one-time free editorial blurb. The length and treatment will vary from publication to publication and the smaller ones will generally give you the most favorable arrangement. Your best bet is to ask for this type of coverage in the form of a review.

Watch Your Ad Backside

When placing your ad, it is best to specify that yours does not back up to one with a coupon on it. If the reader clips the coupon, he might be clipping the most valuable part of your message. It's another one of those problems you must be aware of in order to avoid.

Frequency of Your Ad

Contrary to what many self-styled advertising experts claim, frequency of an ad tends to decrease its pulling power. I have run more than 200 full page ads and have found it almost always to be true. If your ad's first appearance fails to pull in twice

- 83-A -

Corporation Book Is A Best Seller

When businessman/author Ted Nicholas wrote his runaway best selling book, "How To Form Your Own Corporation Without a Lawyer For Under $50.00" he realized that it would aid many independent and small businessmen in forming their own corporations while saving money. What he didn't realize was the nationwide popularity and booming sales that would come.

Soon to enter its 6th printing, "the Corporation book," as it's known in the industry, has sold over 300,000 copies. Over 6,000 corporations having been formed as a direct result of the book. This is easily measured because the book contains a complete set of tear-out forms which the reader can use to form his own corporation.

"Why didn't somebody think of this before?" says one reviewer. "The book does exactly what it says it does — tells you how to form a corporation yourself for under $50."

Ted Nicholas gained his experience in the field during an 18 year business career. During that period he started some 17 corporations, many of them successful; a few not so successful. But, it was the frequent process of incorporating that opened Ted's eyes to the simple fact that the incorporation procedure was a very simple one, often performed by his attorney's competent legal secretary. Thus, the idea for the book was born.

The book explains the three forms of ownership (corporate, individual proprietorship and partnership) and lists their lawyer-created advantages and disadvantages in terms of legal liabilities and tax rates. Those who decide they are best off incorporating can easily do so using the perforated tear-out forms in the back of the book.

Some of the features in this best selling book include sections on:

- How you can incorporate without *any* capital requirement.
- The many *personal* tax benefits of incorporating.
- How a *professional* can benefit from incorporating.
- How to form a "close" or "open" corporation and the difference between them.
- How to save $300 to $1,000 in the formation of the corporation alone.
- An outline of the many situations where you would benefit by incorporating.
- What par and no-par value stock is and which is the most practical.
- Why many "side" businesses and investments should be separately incorporated.
- How to limit *personal* liability.
- SubChapter S Corporations, what they are and how to set one up.
- A state by state list of filing fees for "foreign" corporations.
- Why the State of Delaware is the state most friendly and advantageous to corporations.
- How to actually form a corporation. Step by step complete with the forms to do so.
- Get yourself the same benefits as the largest corporations in America.

As a result of the tremendous success of the book, Ted Nicholas has been swamped with requests from independent salesmen wanting to handle sales of the book as dealers. To accomodate these individuals the publisher, Enterprise Publishing Co., has set up a dealer discount schedule complete with selling ideas.

Interested parties can purchase a copy of the book at $7.95 plus 45¢ for postage and handling and at the same time request dealer discount and sales information. If you elect to sell the book in your area, the purchase price of your first book will be refunded. Send to Enterprise Publishing Co., Dept STE, 1300 Market St., Wilmington, Delaware 19801.

Sample of Free Editorial Coverage

as many sales as the ad cost to run, it is highly unlikely that
a second running will produce more sales. It is my experience
that it will produce less. The moral is, don't waste money trying
to improve sales by running the same ad in the same publication
over and over. In fact, I generally figure an ad will pull tops
on its first appearance in a publication. When I reach a point
where the ad is not producing sales sufficient to offset the ad cost
plus all my other operating expenses, I pull the ad and wait at
least a year before putting it back in that publication. Do not
run marginal ads.

Appear in Alternate Months

If you place your ad in a monthly gardening magazine
for June, I have found it best to wait a month before running the
same ad again in the same publication. First, if it is your initial
appearance in that publication, you will want to wait at least a
month to test the effectiveness of both the ad and the publication.
Secondly, your first appearance tends to "cream the market" --
this is to pull in the hottest prospects. It is best to then wait
a month until the effect of your first ad has subsided somewhat.
If, on the second insertion, you still get a return of three times
the cost of the ad, you will probably want to go with it every

month because you obviously have a book that is in demand and
you are appearing in a publication that reaches the right people.

Your Advertising Plan

Ideally you should always be moving into new publications
with your ads. Of course these untried media are riskier than ones
you have had success with. However, as your sales grow and your
advertising activities pyramid from a single publication or maybe
two, you will soon come to the issue of CREDIT.

Let's say you place ads in a couple of publications to
start out, and these ads pull three to four times the cost. In
such a case it would appear you have a winner. With this evidence
you might seriously consider moving your ad into 20 publications
and use the revenue you receive from anticipated sales to pay for
the cost of the ads. You can see how millionaires are made. And
quickly. But let me also warn you that if you were wrong about
your sales estimate, and sales do not materialize from the additional
ads, you still have to pay for them. And that's how paupers are
made. The key here is to test sufficiently to turn a blind gamble
into a calculated risk.

You will not be able to pyramid your sales in the event
you cannot obtain credit from publications. It is a common practice

among advertisers to maintain an open line of credit with media they use. Insertion orders have space to list other media you have used and paid on time. You can also offer evidence of a bank account and an officer's name to inspire confidence in a balky publication.

As a general rule I like to keep about half my ads in publications I have used before, and half in new markets. When revenue begins to flag, I pull out, wait a year (two ideally) and then go back in the same publication with the same ad. In two years I'm dealing with an almost entirely new market. This plan will not work if you choose a topic such as "Watergate" since that is not a timeless issue. In the two year interim you can write another book.

When to Change Ad Copy

If the ad is pulling successfully, do not change a comma. A good ad is like a perfectly tuned automobile. Any tinkering you do with it is likely only to hurt. I changed just three words once in a very wordy full page ad running in the "New York Times." Changing those three words caused sales to fall from four times cost to one and one half times cost.

On occasions a publication will ask you to change a headline or some element of your ad to better fit in with the appearance or "tone" of the medium. Again, if the ad is successful, don't. If necessary, get out of the publication.

How to Change Ad Copy

The type of ad I have discussed most thus far is the "Factual" variety. In direct mail advertising it is a proven winner, and serves as an excellent basis for launching a potential best selling book. However, there is another variety that you can use as an alternative, especially if your first ad does not pull as well as you would like. I call it the "emotional" approach. Basically you use testimonials from people who have read your book as the substance for the ad itself. The elements you want to stress are subjective rather than the facts you worked with on the first approach. This type of ad approach represents a dramatic departure from the fact ad. Don't be afraid to try it. A very successful mail order book merchandiser named Robert Jameson, President of Performance Dynamics Corporation uses the emotional ad very effectively. Mr. Jameson offers a book on the subject of changing jobs and the importance of finding the right job, and his ads use comments from

people who have had their lives changed by the purchase of his
book.   They tend to emphasize subjective elements such as happiness,
or renewed vigor.

Test Fact vs. Emotion

Many magazines offer a feature whereby you can run two
totally different ads in the same issue of the same publication.
This is called a split run.   They simply stop the press half way
through the press run and change ads.   Thus you can measure the
effectiveness of a factual ad versus an emotional one in the same
magazine and substantially the same audience.   A split run can
often be arranged at no additional cost.   Although, sometimes
there is a small premium that has to be paid.

Coding the Results

It is important to code all your ads, both in print and
in electronic media, in order to be able to determine where your
sales are coming from and in which media dollars are being wisely
and profitably spent.   In print ads, develop an internal coding
system by using a "key number" in the coupon that should appear
at the bottom of all your ads.   On the coupon itself simply print

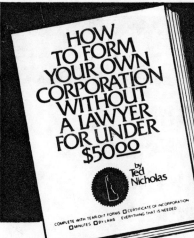

3174 People Become Corporate Presidents

'3174 people from each of the 50 states and most countries throughout the world have already formed their own corporations as a result of How to Form Your own Corporation Without a Lawyer for Under $50. Every one of these corporation presidents is a reference to the book's validity. Most of these corporations are small businesses.

The author is Ted Nicholas, one of the country's outstanding businessmen.

Since March, 1973 over 100,000 copies have been purchased, amounting to nearly a million dollars worth of books. The text has just been fully revised and contains the latest updated information on a state by state basis.

You may be considering incorporating, and surely desire to accomplish this in the most economical way. You are probably seeking methods to *save* tax dollars or *limit* personal liability:

This exciting manual shows you step by step how you can accomplish this for less than $50.00. Included are tearout forms for minutes, bylaws, the actual certificate of incorporation—everything that's needed.

This book is for you if you
- Plan to start a business.
- Own a business.
- Are a partner in a business.
- Desire to raise money through selling shares of stock for a business idea.
- Wish to learn exactly how any corporation is organized to better understand the business world.

It contains everything you've ever wanted to know about corporations.

Here are some of its contents revealed:
- How you can incorporate with absolutely no capital.
- How to limit liability to just the investment in business.
- How to operate anonymously for maximum privacy.
- How to form a nonprofit corporation.
- How to enjoy the many personal tax benefits of incorporation.
- How to legally incorporate without hiring a lawyer.
- How a single individual can be President, Treasurer, Vice-president, Secretary. You can be a one man corporation!

Save $300.00 to as much as $3,000 on the formation of the corporation.

Here is what just a few of the company Presidents that have used the book have to say:

"Your book . . . made it possible . . . to compete in the 'corporate' world. I have recommended your book . . ."—S. Steve Dounis, President, Plaka Records

". . . helps to create a corporation without the . . . high legal fees . . ."—President, Torch Inc., North Carolina

". . . clear, concise, and enlightening, it opens to the 'little guy' . . . new dimensions of business opportunities."—Stu Sinclair, President, CWCA INC., Ohio

"I have found your corporation services to be quite useful and have recommended your services to an international loan market . . ."—Dan H. Brown, II, President, American Trustee and Loan Association, Maryland

". . . would recommend it very highly to anyone wishing to incorporate." —Allyn T. Gallant, President, A. T. Gallant & Co., Inc., California

"Excellent—The Only Way—I Recommend It For All Up And Coming Capitalists."—Roger C. Brown, President, RCB International, Inc., Kentucky

". . . . highly informative. Saved me expense and time."—Curtis S. Jenkins, President, NATCO International Corp., Colorado

". . . complete and helpful in every way."—Les Tiller, President, American Enterprises, Inc., Illinois

". . . a boon to the small man . . . simple to follow . . . savings in fees and costs are tremendous."—Nancy Y. Zepernick, President, NYZ Enterprises, Inc., Virginia

"Well satisfied . . . cost was exactly as represented."—President, Automated Business Information Inc., New York

". . . invaluable to any one . . . in the Corporation World."
—Gordon M. Towns, President, A.U.L.L. Inc., Arkansas

". . . most under-priced available anywhere. Prior to obtaining a copy we'd spent 50 times that amount—with disappointing results."
—Howard Jacobs, President, Omnitron Inc., Canada

READERS COMMENTS From Unsolicited Letters In Our Files:

"Thank you the kindness you have rendered me."
—W. W. B., Terre Haute, Indiana

"Reread important parts again . . . worth many times purchase price."
—J. J., Sunbury, Pennsylvania

"Your book was Excellent! We intend to incorporate within the next few days."—C. B., Lindhurst, N.Y.

"Thank you for writing a book like this. People like myself need it."
—W. B., Grandview, Idaho

"Just want to say thanks . . . Received my copy . . . am very happy with it."—D. J., Houston, Texas

"Outstanding and eye-opening book."—T. J. T., Alexandria, Va.

"Got to admit you've done a superb job . . . my compliments."
—A. W. B., Ararat, N.C.

"Well written . . . informative . . . astounded at rapidity."
—P. B., San Francisco, Ca.

"Book . . . is tops . . . would recommend it to others."
—R. H. W., Carpinteria, Ca.

REVIEWERS COMMENTS

"Handy book . . . Describes in laymen's terms how to proceed . . . Old American spirit lives."—San Francisco Chronicles

"Tells how to incorporate . . . without capital . . . limits personal liability."—New England Business Journal

"Anyone thinking of incorporating . . . should not skip any pages."
—Sacramento Bee

"My attorney, Ralph Benson, is boosting book."—Book Ends n' Odds

"Step by step instructional manual"—Los Angeles Herald Examiner

"One attorney who read it said he'd like his secretary to use it for quick reference."—Delaware Today

"Even for one-man business with little or no capital."
—Home Office Report

"Solid piece of work."—Corporation Dept. official

"For those tired of paying what can amount to thousands in legal fees. One of the best 'How to' books we have seen."—Corporate Finance Newsletter

IRONCLAD GUARANTEE If you are not completely satisfied with the book after you have it for 10 days you may return to for a full refund. To get your copy order now. Fill out coupon below. Tax deductible. Immediate shipment.

TO: ENTERPRISE PUBLISHING CO., INC.
1000 Oakfield Lane, Dept.
Wilmington, Del. 19810

Please send me _____ copies of HOW TO FORM YOUR OWN CORPORATION WITHOUT A LAWYER FOR UNDER $50.00 at $9.95 each, plus 45c postage and handling. It is my understanding that if I am not completely satisfied with the book after 10 days of receipt, I can return the book undamaged for a full refund.

☐ check enclosed   ☐ master charge   ☐ carte blanche   ☐ bankamericard

No. _____   Expiration Date _____   ☐ Diner's Club

NAME (Please Print)_____

ADDRESS _____

CITY_____ STATE _____ ZIP _____

Signature _____

All books sent 4th class. For faster delivery add:
☐ 80c SP. Del.   ☐ $2.25 U.S. Air   ☐ $4.25 Fgn. Air

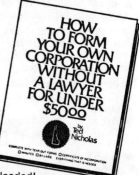
21

Enterprise Publishing Co.

Summary of Advertising Results thru 8/31/75

Title: How To Form Your Own Corporation......

	Key #	Publication	Issue Date	Net Cost	$ Sales	Number of Orders
1	AS-323	American Scientist	Sept/Oct '74	580.55	$1480	97
2	NP-324	National Public Accountant	Sept '74	276.25	554.40	66
3	HI-341	Holiday Inn	Jan/Feb '75	1423.75	230.160	274
4	SO-342	Salesman's Opportunity	Nov '75	964.75	2368.80	282
5	MM-345	Money Making Opportunities	March '75	1198.50	1478.40	176
6	HE-347	Human Events	Jan '75	304.04	453.60	54
7	WP-349	Wall St. Journal	2-11-75	1342.32	1780.80	212
8	HI-351	Holiday Inn	April/May '75	3846.25	430.080	512
9	WS-355	Wall St. Journal	2-25-75	357.04	444.520	53
10	B-363	Barrons	3-16-75	413.38	798.-	95
11	R-368	Reason	May '75	62.-	117.60	14
12	HI-378	Holiday Inn	Jun/July '75	3846.25	4670.40	556
13	MW-389	Moneysworth	6-9-75	1815.11	341.880	467
14	MW-397	Moneysworth	7-7-75	1852.-	3301.20	393
15	IO-322	Income Opportunities	May '75	1398.25	2470.-	175
16	SU-312	Success Unlimited	April '75	952.-	1108.80	132
17	NB-306	Nation's Business	April '05	3641.80	473.760	564
18	MW-307	Moneysworth	3-31-75	1852.-	488.660	582
19						
20						

	Initials	Date
Prepared By		
Approved By		

COLUMN WRITE ®

Sample of Ledger Page Coding Results of Ads

Evaluation of Sales Results from Magazine and Newspaper Ads

Key Code

A - Very Profitable   C - Broke Even
B - Modestly Profitable   D - Lost Money

A
Salesman's Opportunity
Specialty Salesman
Money Making Opportunities
Pasttimes
Penthouse
Nation's Business
Esquire
U.S. News & World Report
Wall Street Journal
New York Times
Capitalist Reporter
Barrons
Carte Blanche
Holiday Inn
Signature
Reason
Human Events
Financial World
National Review
American Scientist
Scientific American
Los Angeles Times
Intellectual Digest

B
Income Opportunities
Success Unlimited
Franchise Journal
Sparetime
Fortune
Business Week
Science Mechanics
American Legion
Braniff Place
TWA Ambassador
Northliner
Better Investing
Insight
National Public Accountant

C
Guide to Earning Extra Income
Popular Mechanics
Playboy
True
Forbes
Money
VFW Magazine
National Observer
Army Times
Empire State Mason
Chicago Tribune

D
Free Enterprise
TV Guide
Newsweek
California Business
Time
Dun's Review
Moose
Delta Sky
Future
Single
Advertising Age
Psychology Today
Dallas Newspaper
Miami Newspaper
Houston Chronicle
San Francisco Chronicle

the word (or abbreviation) "department" followed by a number.
E.g. Dept. 1. You can use the number "1" to designate a publication
like "Farm Journal." Then use number "2" for "Organic Farming"
and "3" for "Farm Monthly" and so on. By keeping a running tally of
the number of sales you are pulling with each ad in each publication,
you will never waste money by continuing marginal ads.

Advantages of Mail Order Selling

For some reason many authors are enamoured by the thought
of having their book stocked on the shelves of bookstores. There
is nothing wrong with that thought, but it certainly is not the
only way to sell books. And it can be argued persuasively that
it is not even the best way.

While it might do an author's ego some good to have his
work carried in bookstores, it does not necessarily do his bank
account any good at all. In general, it is best to promote your
book yourself using mail order as your main distribution source, and
when sales are built up to the point of creating some "demand pull",
then you can approach bookstores, using procedures I will describe
shortly.

Mail order distribution is ideal as a beginning method
since you can do it part time out of your home. You can, in effect,

operate a national or international business with only a modest
investment. There is no discrimination as to sex, age, color or
even mental or physical handicap.

Perhaps the greatest single advantage mail order selling
gives is the ability to compete with Sears Roebuck or General
Motors. All their competitive advantage is boiled down to a page
in a magazine no larger, perhaps, than your ad. And there's a good
chance that your ad can outdraw theirs if you are offering an
interesting book and you write some compelling copy.

In short, mail order selling offers you the chance to
conduct a nationwide, high volume business with little capital
investment.

Another advantage of selling books by mail order is that
they are given a preferential rate. Under the provisions of this
special rate, a book can be shipped anywhere in the United States
for 20¢ for the first pound and 9¢ a pound for each additional
pound or fraction of a pound. Thus for 20¢ you can mail your
one pound book to customers anywhere in the country. This represents
a very economical means of distribution.

When sending paperback books through the mail, you should
be sure to use proper envelopes. The best type is fabricated from
heavyweight 28 pound kraft material, and is at least one half inch

wider and longer than the dimensions of the book itself. For clothbound books I would recommend a padded envelope for added protection.

In order to qualify for the special rate, the envelope
must be marked "Contents: Books -- Special Fourth Class Rate."
Your book must also consist of at least 24 pages and be printed
on both sides.

How to Test a Direct Mail Letter

A direct mail letter is designed to go unsolicited to a
name you have purchased in the form of prospective buyers. Lists
are available by customer category from houses that supply them
for a set fee which is inexpensive; e.g. $25 to $35 per thousand
names. You can get a list of people who have purchased vegetable
seeds by mail during the last year, or a list of people who recently
bought retirement property and might be good candidates for a
garden book. A conversation with representatives of the houses
mentioned in this section of the book might reveal many categories
of potential customers that would not normally occur to you.

The minimum elements of a direct mail letter are: the
letter itself, a separate order coupon, the return reply envelope,
and finally an outer mailing envelope.

ENTERPRISE PUBLISHING CO.   1000 OAKFIELD LANE/WILMINGTON, DELAWARE 19810

NEW BOOK BY TED NICHOLAS

WHERE THE MONEY IS AND HOW TO GET IT

Post-Publication Offer

You are one of the selected purchasers of Mr. Ted Nicholas' best selling book, HOW TO FORM YOUR OWN CORPORATION WITHOUT A LAWYER FOR UNDER $50.00, who is receiving this offer.

Mr. Nicholas has completed a new book. This beautifully hardbound book contains more than 2,000 sources of capital!

More than any other book on raising business capital, it will tell you where to raise the money you need to start or expand your business and having zeroed in on a source of funds, how to go about actually raising them.

The author is a brilliant 39 year old who started his own business at 22 with $800. He now has 18 corporations in such diverse fields as real estate, retailing, franchising, confectionery, building design and machinery manufacturing. In his new book he shares his money-raising experience with you.

Selected as one of the outstanding businessmen in the United States in 1964, he was invited to personally meet and consult with the President, the late Lyndon B. Johnson.

His book is presently being sold to the general public at $10.00. (plus $.45 postage and handling).

The price to you is just $7.95 and we will pay postage. You save $2.50!

If you are seeking capital for you business, for a business idea, scholarship funds, or a research grant, this book is a must. It is a comprehensive manual of capital sources and how to go about successfully raising money.

The book lists more than 2,000 money sources anxious to advance you the money you need. Billions of dollars are available -- capitalization from $500 to $5,000,000.

Some of the topics discussed are:

How to approach any capital source.

The difference between venture and adventure capital.

(Cont'd.)

WHERE THE MONEY IS AND HOW TO GET IT   Page 2

Special advantages for Vietnam veterans seeking funds
to start a business.

Getting long-term financing from your state to expand
your business -- build a new plant, buy machinery.

Using other people's money to build your business.

How to franchise your business and raise capital.

Negotiating a loan from any of 96 listed commercial
banks which make business loans.

How to sell stock in your corporation to raise capital.

How to conduct a private stock offering without registration.

How to prepare a public offering in your corporation.

How to conduct an interstate offering of stock.

A list of 103 stock underwriting firms who can take your
company "public" even if it is just starting in business.

A list of the 100 largest finance companies that often
provide financing when banks will not.

More than 1,600 tax-exempt foundations that have assets
over $500,000. The most valuable list ever compiled.

How to advertise in your local newspaper to attract
investors.

227 Small Business Investment Companies, licensed by the
federal government, with name, address, phone number, and
individual to contact.

Remember, this offer is limited. It expires on August 30th.

This book is offered on an ironclad money-back guarantee.

You save $2.50 per copy if you act now. If you are not entirely
satisfied within 10 days of receipt, you may return the book for a
full refund.

A postage-paid envelope is enclosed for your convenience.

Sincerely,

Doris Palmer

Doris Palmer

P.S. Remember, if this book is not everything I say it is and worth
to you many times its purchase price, just return it for a full
refund.

The Sales Brochure

In addition to the elements just mentioned, you might also enclose a sales brochure to some particularly good prospects. I have had great success with a four page brochure done on an 11" x 17" sheet. It is printed on both sides and folded down to 8½" x 11". The brochure information basically follows the formula for the full page ad and incorporates much of the same information. For a rich feel, I use green or brown ink on a blue or buff colored stock. This gives an appearance of much color but at little or no extra cost since it is still only a one-color printing job. In quantities of 5,000 this type brochure costs Enterprise Publishing Company about 7¢ each.

Making Your Test

When making a direct mail test, you find yourself testing both the letter itself and the list you bought. The test, of course, is to measure whether or not the letter brings in sales beyond the cost of the mailing and the list. To be meaningful your test must include at least 1,000 to 3,000 names.

You should try to purchase your list by "computer printout." These will be in zip code order enabling them to be

"I WAS QUOTED A PRICE OF $1,000 BY A LAWYER FOR EACH OF 3 CORPORATIONS I WANTED TO FORM. THIS BOOK SAVED ME ALMOST $3,000." J. S., Business Owner

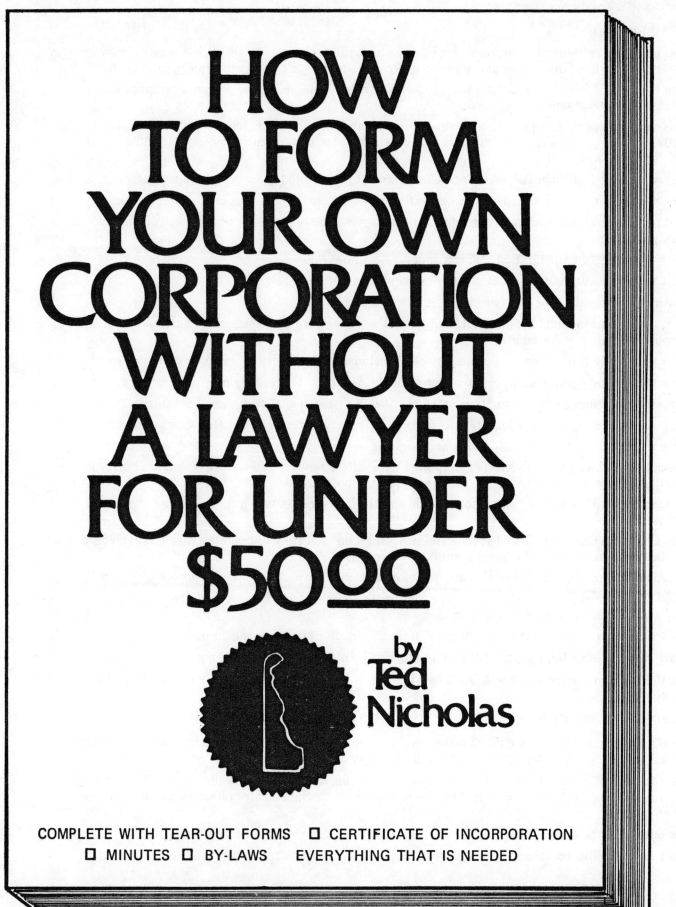

DEAR FRIEND:

You may have considered incorporating. I'm sure you want to accomplish this in the most economical way. You may already be in business and are looking for ways to <u>save</u> tax dollars or <u>limit</u> personal liability.

You can benefit from this manual if you are planning a one man business if you are associated with a partner or are the owner of a large company.

This exciting report shows you step by step how you can accomplish this for <u>less than $50.00.</u> It <u>contains</u> <u>tear</u> <u>out</u> <u>forms</u> for everything that is needed! This includes minutes, by-laws, and the actual certificate of incorporation!

It is written by Ted Nicholas* – Business Consultant. It is presented in simple, clear language.

You'll learn of the many benefits of incorporating either an existing business or one that is planned.

Just by filling out and mailing the attached card, a copy will be reserved for you with a full money back guarantee.

Some of the features of this best selling manual are, sections on:

How you can incorporate without <u>any</u> capital requirement.

The many <u>personal</u> tax benefits of incorporating.

How a corporation limits the personal liability for the owner(s) of a business, to the investment in the corporation. (Except for taxes)

How to actually form a corporation step by step. Included are instructions on completing the forms.

How to own and operate a corporation anonymously if desired. This assures maximum privacy.

How to form a non profit corporation. How to utilize tax "gimmicks" to personal advantage.

Find out why lawyers charge huge fees for incorporating services even when often times they prefer not to.

How a *"professional"* can benefit from incorporating.

Learn how and why you can legally incorporate without the services of a lawyer. There is a fallacy in that most people feel it is necessary to have a lawyer to incorporate.

How to form an "open" or "close" corporation and the difference between them. Report contains tear out forms.

Sub Chapter S Corporations. What they are. How to set one up. How to operate a business as a corporation, yet be taxed on individual tax rates if more advantageous.

Learn about the many dangers and hazards of not incorporating partnerships and proprietorships.

What a Registered Agent is. How assistance is provided to individuals who incorporate. The most economical company to use. A complete section on this.

How to cut out all fees of the "middle man" normally involved in forming a corporation.

How to save from $300 to over $1,000 in the formation of the corporation alone!

What a *"foreign"* corporation is. A State by State list of the filing fees involved in registering a "foreign" corporation.

Learn how a corporation can sell its stock to raise capital at any time.

How a single individual can hold all offices in a corporation. There is no need to have anyone involved except a single stockholder although, of course, as many as desired can be included.

How to arrange for any stock sold to an investor in a corporation to be tax deductible to the investor's personal income in the event of loss. This makes the sale of stock in a corporation far more attractive to an investor.

An outline of the many situations where an individual would benefit by incorporating.

How to legally incorporate and sell stock in a corporation without "registering" the stock.

Over 100,000 satisfied customers!

What par and no-par value stock is and which is the most practical.

How an existing, unincorporated business anywhere in the United States can benefit by incorporating. Also included are the steps to take after incorporating.

The reasons why most of the corporations listed on the American and New York Stock Exchanges incorporate in Delaware — the State most friendly to corporations — and how you can have the same benefits as the largest corporations in America.

What to do if you are already incorporated in another state and want to take advantage of incorporating in Delaware.

Learn why many "side" business and investments should be separately incorporated.

This is what enthusiastic Reviewers are saying:

> "Handy book . . . Describes in laymen's terms how to proceed. Old American spirit lives."
>
> San Francisco Chronicle

> "Tells how to incorporate . . . without capital . . . limits personal liability"
>
> New England Business Journal

> "Step by step instructional manual"   Los Angeles Herald Examiner

> "Anyone thinking of incorporating . . . should not skip any pages."
>
> Sacramento Bee

It works. Thousands of people from every state in the U. S. have already used it to form corporations.

Just complete the card below and your manual will be promptly mailed to you.

If at the end of a ten day free trial period you are not completely satisfied, simply return the report and your money will be promptly refunded.*

Sincerely,

Dale Palmer

Dale Palmer
Assistant to the President

P.S. Due to new tax law, it is more advantageous than ever before to incorporate. Tax rate is only 20% for income up to $50,000 and 22% instead of 48% on next $25,000 of income! (effective for year 1975)

 *We participate in arbitration for business and customers through the Better Business Bureau of Delaware.

DEPT. BB

Please send me _____ copies of "HOW TO FORM YOUR OWN CORPORATION WITHOUT A LAWYER FOR UNDER $50.00" by Ted Nicholas at $9.95 each, plus $.45 postage and handling.

☐ I prefer to have _____ copies of deluxe special limited Library Edition of above book, bound in cloth, gold embossing @ $14.95 each.

If I am not completely satisfied with the book after 10 days of receipt, I can return the book undamaged for a full refund.

☐ check enclosed   ☐ Master Charge   ☐ Bank Americard
☐ Carte Blanche   ☐ Diner's Club

Credit Card # _____ Exp. Date _____

Signature _____
(Please print or type)

NAME _____

ADDRESS _____

CITY _____ STATE _____ ZIP____

For Faster Delivery: Add   ☐ 80¢ Special Delivery   ☐ $2.25 U. S. Air   ☐ $4.25 Foreign Air

Enterprise Publishing Company, Inc.
1300 Market Street
Wilmington, Delaware 19801

COMMENTS FROM READERS
What Readers of the Manuscript Report have Said...

"I want to buy several copies for my clients," — Insurance Executive

"If I'd known about this I would have incorporated years ago," — Salesman

"This report is a handy reference for me." — Lawyer

"The author is experienced in the corporate world, giving him the qualifications to write this book." — Judge

"Fantastic! Do you want a partner?" — Lawyer

"Good idea. Brings the concept of being incorporated within the reach of anyone." — Artist

"I was quoted a price of $1,000 each for 3 corporations I want to form! This report saved me almost $3,000!" — Business Owner

"Excellent! Written so that anyone can understand it." — Secretary

"Takes the mystery out of forming a corporation." — Printer

"Very well written. Will encourage many small business to incorporate." — Housewife

"Great idea! I'd be glad to promote it for a piece of the action." — Advertising Executive

"Should be in every business library." — Executive

"Will be forming two new corporations in January using this method." — Publisher

"Well written. Will eventually produce more business for lawyers." — Lawyer

---

Permit No. 389
Wilmington
Delaware
19803

BUSINESS REPLY MAIL
No postage stamp necessary if mailed in the United States

POSTAGE WILL BE PAID BY

ENTERPRISE PUBLISHING CO., INC.
1300 Market Street
Wilmington, Delaware 19801

sent fourth class mail at 6.5¢ apiece. Statistics, by the way, indicate that despite popular opinion, people read fourth class mail every bit as much as they do first class.

As an indication of just how lucrative selling literature by mail can be, I know a man in Japan who operates out of a loft sending out 50,000 letters to the U.S. daily. He drives a Rolls Royce and has more money than he could ever spend.

He sells reports of about 60 pages for $4 - $6 on a variety of subjects from "An Unusual Diet from the Orient" to "77 Products for Import." He tests a list, then "rolls out" with it going to an ever enlarging number of buyers.

The unusual oriental postmark is almost irresistible to people in the U. S. who receive it. He looks to making $20 to $30 profit per 1000 names. And at 50,000 letters a day, that comes to $1000 - $1500 daily profit.

I use this example simply to show that you can use direct mail exclusively and be extremely successful at it. Some types of subject matter might be best handled by direct mail especially if media are reluctant to run your ads. Some political books and others of a highly controversial nature might fall into such a category.

WHERE AND HOW TO SELL

Selling to Bookstores

While mail order selling will probably offer the best potential for merchandising your book, you shouldn't overlook the 13,000 book dealers in the U.S.

R. R. Bowker Company's "Literary Market Place" can put you in touch with dozens of wholesalers. Their "American Book Trade Directory" tells who to contact and outlines particular interests of every bookstore and wholesaler in the U.S. and Canada.

As a general rule, bookstores and libraries tend to make purchases through wholesale book distributors. I have included the names and addresses of some wholesalers who will be able to help merchandise your book through retail shops. Send the wholesaler a letter describing your book and let him get back in touch with you.

However, if you are the type who likes to do things yourself, you can contact bookstores and department stores directly. Perhaps the best direct approach is to load up the trunk of your car and simply start off. If you call for an appointment, it is easy to be put off by a secretary. However, if you show up, book in hand, ready to do business, you are bound to make some sales.

WHOLESALE PRICE AND DISCOUNT SCHEDULE

This best selling nationally advertised book should be in the
Business Section of your shop.

HOW TO FORM YOUR OWN CORPORATION WITHOUT A LAWYER FOR UNDER $50
by Ted Nicholas

Bookstores	Retail Price	Discount	Price per Book
1-2 copies	$7.95	20%	$6.35 (plus 23¢ shipping)
3-9 copies	$7.95	30%	$5.55 postpaid
10 & over	$7.95	40% *	$4.75 postpaid

Special Hardbound Library Edition

	$12.50	--	$12.50

This rapid seller is a must. It offers answers in this age of
tight money and inflation, its title is -

WHERE THE MONEY IS AND HOW TO GET IT   by Ted Nicholas

1-2 copies	$10.00	20%	$8.00 (plus 30¢ shipping)
3-9 copies	$10.00	30%	$7.00 postpaid
10 & over	$10.00	40% *	$6.00 postpaid

* maximum discount

Terms: Bills must be paid within 30 days of invoice date. Otherwise
NO discounts will be allowed.

Please supply trade references with whom you are on open account
and one bank reference. Otherwise please submit payment with
order.

All books (undamaged) are fully returnable for 120 days from
purchase for full credit.

It has been my experience that bookstore owners and operators are down to earth people who enjoy talking shop. The standard discount is 40% of the selling price. You can work your own deals from there depending upon how badly you want the exposure in any particular book or department store. Don't avoid the large department stores because you fear the managers won't talk to you. These establishments sell an incredible number of books, and their book department managers frequently have more time to sit and discuss your book than a small shop operator who must divide his time and energy among a multiplicity of duties.

You do, in fact, have to try harder than sales representatives for the high overhead conventional publishers whose names are well known and whose book stable has perhaps received heavy publicity. But your personal effort, coupled with your knowledge of your own work, gives you a competitively enthusiastic edge no mere salesman for another's book can match.

Selling to Schools

Schools represent one of the most massive markets in the U.S. Currently two million teachers select not only textbooks, but related source books as well in planning their courses.

Computerized lists have made possible the fine tuning of
teachers' names with their specific subject areas and student age
levels.

I have included a couple of sources for such lists:
Educational Directory, 126 Blaine Avenue, Marion, Ohio, 43302.
This firm's strength is its breakdown of college faculty into very
specific subject categories.

The best mailing lists for schools are available from R.
R. Bowker, 1180 Avenue of the Americas, New York, New York 10036.

Special Events

Book and department stores are not the only outlets for
selling your book. For a work on the subject of organic gardening,
flower shops, greenhouses, health food stores, or even hardware
stores could all be potential and logical places to select and
purchase such a book.

Once you begin to think in terms of marketing your work,
all sorts of other possibilities will become obvious to you.
Garden clubs always need speakers, and what better opportunity to
offer autographed copies of your book. County fairs, farmers'

markets, and even conventions and trade shows offer splendid opportunities for setting up a small booth. It has been my experience that the contacts you make at events like these are even more important than the number of books you sell. You'll get new ideas and new perspectives for merchandising your book.

Fulfillment of Book Orders
Post Office Box or Street Address

There are differing views on whether a Post Office Box is as effective as a street mailing address in a mail order ad. While a few publishers use a Post Office Box, I prefer a street address. It suggests that your company has more substance and stability than a numbered box. If you choose this approach you can use your home address, an office, or mail forwarding service if you prefer.

Prior to your receiving orders for your book, carefully organize procedures for filling them. It is most discouraging to a book buyer when there is a long delay in shipment. Prompt shipments within 48 hours are desirable for a successful operation.

Some suggestions are:

1. To protect your book against damage during shipment use a cushioned bag or sturdy carton. Many printers and/or stationery supply houses stock them.

2. For addressing to your customers use a pre-
gummed 4 part address label (original and 3 copies, 33
labels on a sheet). Use one for your customer's address,
the second to keep a list of your customers to accumulate
for list rental purposes, and the others for possible
mailings to your customers and for extra file copies. Type
on the label the Department code number from the coupon ad
that has been answered and the date of shipment for
reference in the event there is correspondence about the
order.

3. If a customer writes and tells you he has not
received his book within 4-6 weeks of shipment, send
another book at no cost to him. The Post Office does
fail to deliver on occasion.

4. Have your company name and address and the words
"Books - Special 4th Class Rate" printed directly on
your mailing carton or shipping bag or on a printed gummed
label. You will thus qualify for this low cost postal rate.

5. Keep inventory in your house or rent a warehouse
until your printings become large, then have your printer
stock your books. You will pay a small storage fee for
this. Many printers will fill orders for you if you wish.

All you need do is supply them with the prepared address labels of your customers.

No matter how large you become, you probably want to handle air mail and special delivery orders yourself and keep a small inventory on hand.

6. When you begin doing a volume business, you will need help in the important fulfillment function. You can handle this in several ways.

    a. Hire on a salaried payment basis.

    b. Hire part-time hourly people who work out of their homes.

    c. Hire a self-employed independent contractor.

We utilize a combination of these methods with the heaviest emphasis on an independent contractor. She is a capable person, in her own incorporated business (secretarial service), and who works out of her home, thereby assuring her maximum flexibility in setting hours for her work as well as personal and family life. She is paid on a per order basis and has a staff of hourly helpers who are housewives working part time to supplement family income. She, of course, benefits as the business grows and is rewarded in accordance with her productivity and efficiency.

If this appeals to you, you could work out such an arrangement. A good place to secure such a candidate is by running a classified ad in your local paper. Also watch ads under services offered and under the category-situation wanted, female or male.

Some suggestions on an incentive pay scale for an independent contractor would be as follows: typing - hourly at $3.00, opening mail - 5¢ for each envelope, typing labels - 5¢ each, special delivery orders - 25¢ each, bookstore orders - 35¢ each, trips to post office or bank - $1.00-$2.00 each, etc. You can establish your own arrangements that best suit your needs and the general pay scale of the area in which you live.

How to Sell Paperback Rights to Your Book

If the results of your initial advertising and promotion efforts are positive, you might want to contact a conventional publisher with your sales figures. The advantage of such an arrangement is that you can receive the "big bucks" advertising and promotion support that will likely catapult you and your book to quick success. The disadvantage is that you will have to share the profits with the conventional publisher.

Selling Foreign Rights

Again, after you have some idea of your sales success in this country, you might want to contact a book dealer who handles

foreign rights about marketing your book in other countries.
Thousands of authors add to both their finances and prestige through
this method. I have found that two criteria should be met before
you attempt sales abroad. First, "Is your book salable in this
country?" and second, "Does it lend itself to use by readers in
other countries?" For example, a book on How to Obtain a U.S.
Divorce would not be much good to international readers. However,
a book on the Secrets of Organic Gardening might well be popular
anywhere in the world.

Join the Better Business Bureau

To help establish credibility in the community and with
your customers, it is a good idea to join the Better Business
Bureau. People feel better dealing with a firm that is accepted
by the business community. Enterprise Publishing Company has been
a member since its inception and I can heartily recommend the
organization.

Keeping Records

The best advice I can give you on keeping records is to
start out right. Do it correctly from the very beginning of your

business, and you will not get in trouble. The temptation is to begin paying bills and stick receipts in desk drawers with the idea that, "I'll get organized as soon as I have some time." That will never happen, at least not before you have had to beg an accountant to put your long outdated and incomplete records into accounting language. If you procrastinate on the matter of record keeping for even a short time, it will cost dearly to have an accountant piece together the financial history of your business.

However, if you start right, you can hire an accountant who moonlights, and for very little money maintain a set of books that will tell you exactly where your business venture stands at any given point in time.

The simplest method I've found for record keeping is a "one-write" system. With this, you write a check and the check is automatically posted to your ledger through a carbon. You also write the address on the check and use a handy window envelope. The system I use is put out by the Safeguard Company. You can find them in your Yellow Pages.

If you use this system, and faithfully enter all the bills you pay, you will have the basis for a good bookkeeping system.

Sample of "One Write" Bookkeeping System

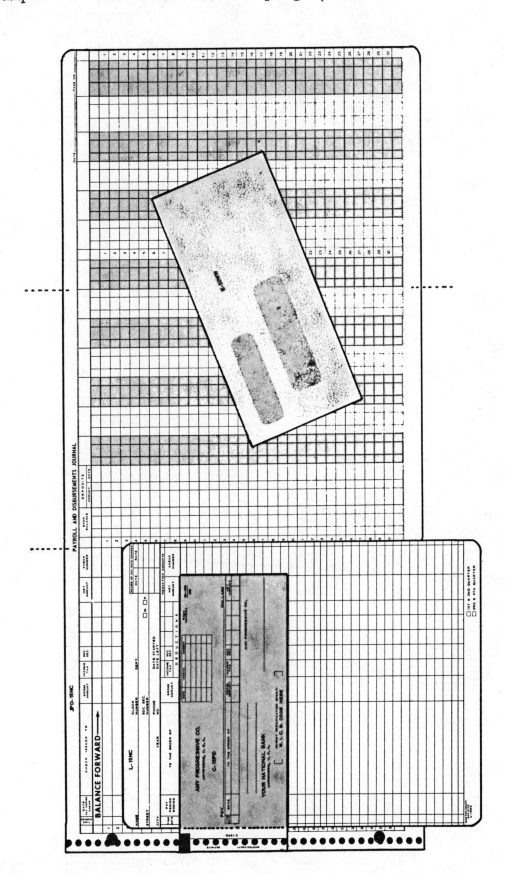

Your Mailing List as a Valuable Property

A side benefit of developing a mailing list of your own is that many others will pay handsomely to use your list for selling their products. I have made $4,000 a month income from simply selling my lists. If you develop a mailing list of organic gardeners, you can potentially sell the list to mail order merchandisers of seeds, garden tools, outdoor clothing and so on.

How to Keep Informed

If you do not already subscribe to one of the writers' magazines, I would suggest you do so. They contain tips not only on writing and development of the craft, but also information on marketing your work. I recommend:

The Writer
8 Arlington Street
Boston, Mass. 02116
  Cost,$7 per year

Writer's Digest
22 East 12th Street
Cincinnati, Ohio 45210
  Cost, $4 per year

Another way of keeping abreast of developments in the writing and publishing field is to join a writers' association. Here are two you can contact directly for information about membership:

The National Writers' Club
745 Sherman Street
Denver, Colo. 80203

Author's League of America
234 West 44th Street
New York, New York 10036

SUMMARY

In conclusion, I would like to leave you with a thought that probably would have made you quit reading if I had put it in the foreword section of this book. It is, "Your first self publishing effort really amounts to a darned good dry run for subsequent books." Like most things in life, self publishing gets easier the more you do it. Since publishing is such a totally unfamiliar world to most writers, it takes first-hand immersion in the complete promotion, advertising and merchandising cycle just to become acquainted with the mechanics of the book business. You will learn by your mistakes, and with the help of this book, you should be limited to making small ones in terms of time and money rather than big costly ones.

As you can see, the writing of a best seller represents only a fraction of the total effort required to create one. It is the effort you put in AFTER the book is written that will make that writing effort pay off. Thousands upon thousands of writers choose instead to spend their energies and money packing their manuscript off to publisher after publisher without any real knowledge of the problems that block their paths to success and acceptance.

Still others fall prey to the promises of vanity and subsidy publishers who do part of the work, but leave the most important promotion and advertising undone.

Think back on the effort you put into writing your book. Doesn't it deserve at least that much effort to make it into a paying proposition for you? If so, there should be nothing to stop you from promoting your book to best seller status. I have outlined sources for raising capital if ready cash is a problem. I have given you names and addresses of printers and people involved in all phases of editorial production. I have shown you proven methods of promotion and advertising that have been used not only with my best sellers, but every book that ever sold out of its first printing.

The most important step is the one that only you can take ... it is that first one. I hope you do take it, and I hope the road it starts you down is as pleasant and profitable as the one I have been on for three years now.

Along with my best wishes for your success, I would like to invite you to send me a copy of your book when you have it in print.

Bibliography

Allen, Dorothy and Lewis, "Printing with the Handpress," Van Nostrand-Reinhold. This definitive manual is intended to encourage fine printing through hand craftsmanship.

Anderson, Charles B. and Smith, G. Roysce, 1969, "A Manual on Bookselling," Harmony Books, Division of Crown Publishers. Helpful tips on selling books as seen through the eyes of a bookstore owner.

Arnold, Edmund, "Ink on Paper," Harper. Provides practical, accurate, elementary advice on all phases of printing.

Bailey, Herbert S., Jr. "The Art and Science of Book Publishing." New York: Harper & Row. ("The Torch Book.") Book publishing as seen by a prominent university press publisher.

Bowker, "American Book Trade Directory." Issued yearly listing more than 16,000 booksellers, publishers and wholesalers in the United States and Canada and gives information about each.

Bowker, "Literary Market Place." Issued yearly providing vital information of practical use to the publishing and literary trades.

Colby, Jean Poindexter, "Writing, Illustrating and Editing Children's Books," New York: Hastings House. About producing children's books.

Congoli, John, "Photo Offset Fundamentals," 1960. Good overview of the subject.

Copperud, Roy H., "A Dictionary of Usage and Style," 1964. Tips from a teacher and former newspaperman.

Downs, Robert B., "Books that Changed the World." New York: New American Library. Cloth ed., American Library Association.

Dustbooks, "Directory of Small Magazine/Press Editors." Lists small press editors with descriptions about each.

Feininger, Andreas, "The Complete Photographer," 1965. A good basic manual by a LIFE photographer.

Flesh, Rudolph, "The Art of Readable Writing," 1949. A basic discussion of readability ideas and theories.

Foster, Joanna, "Pages, Pictures and Print: A Book in the Making," New York: Harcourt Brace Jovanovich. A specialist in children's books writes entertainingly about how a book is produced.

Fulton, Len and James Boyer May."Dustbooks". Gives comprehensive information about small publishers.

Goodman, Joseph V., "How to Publish, Promote and Sell Your Book," 1970, Adams Press. Hits the highlights of producing a book yourself.

Guinzburg, Harold K., et al. "Books and the Mass Market," Urbana, Ill.: University of Illinois Press. The late president of Viking Press writes about the marketing of books.

Gunning, "Technique of Clear Writing," McGraw-Hill, New York

Hackett, Alice Payne, "Seventy Years of Best Sellers," New York: R. R. Bowker Co. A fascinating account of book sales and reading habits in America from 1895 to 1965.

Haight, Anne Lyon, "Banned Books," New York: R. R. Bowker Co. An account of more than three hundred books that have been banned during the last twenty-five centuries.

Harrington, Harry F., "Pathways to Print," 1931. Dated, but basic ideas still sound.

Heinemann, William, "The Hardships of Publishing," 1893. Gives interesting perspective to show times have not changed much for authors.

Henderson, Bill, "The Publish-It-Yourself Handbook," Pushcart Press, 1973. A good collection of firsthand experiences by people who have self published.

Huenefeld, John, "How to Make Money Publishing Books," Vinebrook Productions, Inc. Great if you plan to publish others' works.

Hunt, Cecil, "How to Write a Book," 1952.

Karbo, Joe, "The Lazy Man's Way to Riches," 1973, This book explains techniques in sales, advertising and promotion in very understandable language.

Klare, George R. "The Measurement of Readability." 1963.

Knopf, Alfred A. "Publishing Then and Now: 1912-1964. New York: New York Public Library. Reminiscences by a famous American publisher.

Lee, Marshall, "Bookmaking: The Illustrated Guide to Design and Production." Good for someone who needs to deal with printers and publishers but lacks general knowledge.

Lehmann-Haupt, Hellmut, et al. "The Book in America." New York: R. R. Bowker Co. A history of the production and selling of books in the United States.

Lieberman, J. Ben, "Printing as a Hobby," 1963. Small, easy to read book on basic typography.

Link, Henry C., and Arthur Hopf, "People and Books: A Study of Reading and Book-Buying Habits," 1946.

McMurtrie, Douglas C. "The Book: The Story of Printing and Bookmaking," New York: Oxford University Press. An account of how a book is produced.

Melcher, D. and N. Larrick, "The Printing & Production Handbook," McGraw. Very helpful and complete book for those not knowledgeable in advertising and direct mail techniques.

Morrill, Sibley S., "The Self Publishing Writer," 1018 Lincoln Ave., San Jose, Calif., 95125. A quarterly journal with each issue containing about five articles of interest to self publishing authors. Subscription price $7.50 per year.

Mott, Frank L. "Golden Multitudes." New York: R. R. Bowker Co. Favorite books in the U.S. from 1662 to 1945.

Mumby, Frank A., and Norrie, Ian. "Publishing and Bookselling: A History from the Earliest Times to the Present Day." New York: R. R. Bowker Co. The standard English work on the subject.

Munson, Gorham, "The Written Word, How to Write Readable Prose."
    1949.

Nicholas, Ted, "How to Form Your Own Corporation Without A Lawyer
    for Under $50," Enterprise Publishing Co.

Nicholas, Ted, "Where the Money Is and How to Get It.", Enterprise
    Publishing Co.

Nicholson, Margaret, "A Manual of Copyright Practice," Oxford
    University Press, Good straight forward guide on copyright
    fundamentals.

Raeder, Nicholas and Regina Longyear, "The Shoestring Publishers
    Guide," Sol III Publications, Box 751, One Wilton Road, Farmington,
    Maine, 94938. One of the best "How To" books if you plan to
    actually print a book or magazine yourself. Not much help, however,
    on the advertising/promotion end.

Reed, A. W., "The Author-Publisher Relationship," 1946.

Skillin, Marjorie and Robert Gay, "Words Into Type." A manual for
    manuscript preparation including proofreader's marks, style and
    typography.

Smith, Datus C., Jr., "A Guide to Book Publishing," New York: R. R.
    Bowker Co. A guide to the general principles of book publishing.

Smith, Roger H., "The American Reading Public: What It Reads--Why
    It Reads." New York: R. R. Bowker Co. The publishing industry and
    its relationship to what people read.

Stevens, George, "Best Sellers, Are They Born or Made?" 1939.

Strunk, William Jr. and E. B. White, "The Elements of Style,"
    Famous New York writer and his professor discuss good writing.

Tebbel, John, "A History of Book Publishing in the United States,"
    3 vols. New York: R. R. Bowker Co. A definitive history of
    American book publishing.

Uhlan, Edward, "The Rogue of Publishers' Row," Jericho, N.Y.:
    Exposition Press. A publisher defends "vanity" publishing.

University of Chicago Press, "A Manual of Style." The standard
    bearer for writers, printers and editors.

Wolfe, Thomas, "The Story of a Novel," New York: Charles Scribner's
    Sons. The author of "Look Homeward, Angel" talks about his
    writing.

Sample letter when book is returned as undeliverable.

Dear Customer:

    On _____ the book _____

_____ which was sent to you at the

above address was returned to us marked _____

_____ .

    We will mail a second copy to you if you will

please send us an address where you will be assured of

receiving the book.

                    Sincerely,

                    D. M. Palmer (Mrs.)
                    Customer Service

Sample letter on improper credit card purchase.

Dear Customer:

RETURN CREDIT SALES SLIP

Credit Card # _____

Your _____ has been
returned to us with the notation _____.
No doubt this is due to an error either by our typist or by
you when you filled out the coupon ordering the book(s) listed
below.

TITLE   PRICE

However, this is serious as a product has been
obtained without payment. Please forward your correct card
number promptly so this account can be settled. Thank you.

Sincerely,

D. M. Palmer
Credit Manager

P

Sample letter for improper payment of book order.

Dear Customer:

SUBJECT: PRODUCT OBTAINED WITHOUT PAYMENT

Your _____ has been returned to us marked

_____. You ordered the following book(s)

which was shipped to you.

TITLE:_____

_____

We assume this nonpayment is an oversight or an error on

your part. However, this is serious for a product has been obtained

without payment. Please promptly forward the amount owed ($_____)

to avoid credit and legal action by an international collection

agent (TSC Corporation) who handles all our bad checks, payment

defaults, and improper use of credit cards. Thank you.

Sincerely,

D. M. Palmer
Credit Manager

p

Sample letter for book order received without payment.

Dear Customer:

We enclose your order for the following book(s):

TITLE	PRICE	POSTAGE & HANDLING

Please return a check or money order in the amount of _____ along with your order and the book will be promptly mailed to you. We enclose a self-addressed return envelope for your convenience.

Sincerely,

D. M. Palmer (Mrs.)
Customer Service

dp:m

Enclosure

Sample of reply letter for book not received.

Dear Customer:

      We are in receipt of your letter informing us that you have not received the following book you ordered.

      TITLE: _____

      This book was sent _____.
Occasionally the Post Office takes several weeks to deliver books. (NOTE: The fourth class book rate takes longer than first class mail.) If, by _____ you have not received your book, please return this letter to us and enclose your correct address plus a copy of your cancelled check . We will then send you a second copy of the book. Thank you.

                       Sincerely,

                       D. M. Palmer (Mrs.)
                       Customer Service

p

Sample letter to customer on refund request.

                    TITLE: _____

Dear Customer:

        The book that you returned for a refund has been
received. We wish to comply with our policy of making a
prompt refund.

        However, the original address label has been obliterated
or removed. This label has a code containing information regarding
how, when, where and at what price the book was purchased. Since
other companies also sell our books (packaged in our mailers) the
buyer must obtain his refund from the selling company. Also, this
book is drop-shipped for certain mail order firms, and sold through
major credit card organizations.

        If this book was purchased directly from our company,
a photocopy of your cancelled check is required for a cash refund,
or the credit card charge number used, so we may issue a credit
rebate to the charge card company.

                                At your service,

                                D. M. Palmer (Mrs.)
                                Customer Service

p

        NOTE: PLEASE RETURN THIS LETTER WITH YOUR REPLY!

As advertised in the Wall Street Journal, Barrons, National Observer, New York Times, Fortune, Business Week. Nations Business , etc.

How to form your own corporation without a lawyer for under $50.⁰⁰

By Ted Nicholas

You may have considered incorporating. I'm sure you want to accomplish this in the most economical way. You may already be in business and are looking for ways to save tax dollars or limit personal liability.

You can benefit from this report if you are planning a one man business if you are associated with a partner or are the owner of a large company.

This exciting report shows you step by step how you can accomplish this for less than $50.00.

It contains tear-out forms for everything that is needed! This includes minutes, bylaws, and the actual certificate of incorporation!

It is presented in simple, clear language.

You'll learn of the many benefits of incorporating either an existing business or one that is planned.

Some of the features of the 8½ x 11, 30,000 word, 103 page report:

How you can incorporate without any capital requirement with zero capital.

The many personal tax benefits of incorporating.

How a corporation limits the personal liability for the owner(s) of a business, to the investment in the corporation. (Except for taxes)

How to actually form a corporation step by step. Included are instructions on completing the forms.

How to own and operate a corporation anonymously if desired. This assures maximum privacy.

How to form a non profit corporation. How to utilize tax "gimmicks" to personal advantage.

Find out why lawyers charge huge fees for incorporating services even when often times they prefer not to.

Learn how and why you can legally incorporate without the services of a lawyer. There is a fallacy in that most people feel it is necessary to have a lawyer to incorporate.

How to form an "open" or "close" corporation and the difference between them. Report contains tear out forms.

Sub Chapter S Corporations. What they are. How to set one up. How to operate a business as a corporation, yet be taxed on individual tax rates if more advantageous.

Learn about the many dangers and hazards of not incorporating partnerships and proprietorships.

What a Registered Agent is. How assistance is provided to individuals who incorporate. The most economical company to use. A complete section on this.

How to cut out all fees of the "middle man" normally involved in forming a corporation.

IRON CLAD GUARANTEE. If you are not completely satisfied with the book after you have it for 10 days you may return it for a full refund.

COMMENTS FROM READERS

"I want to buy several copies for my clients."–Insurance Executive
"If I'd known about this I would have incorporated years ago." -Salesman
"This report is a handy reference for me."–Lawyer
"The author is experienced in the corporate world, giving him the qualifications to write this book." Judge
"Fantastic! Do you want a partner?" -Lawyer
"Good idea. Brings the concept of being incorporated within the reach of anyone."–Artist
"I was quoted a price of $1,000 each for 3 corporations I want to form! This report saves me almost $3,000!"–Business Owner
"Excellent! Written so that anyone can understand it."–Secretary
"Takes the mystery out of forming a corporation."–Printer
"Very well written. Will encourage many small businesses to incorporate."–Housewife
"Well written. Will eventually produce more business for lawyers."–Lawyer
"Great idea! I'd be glad to promote it for a piece of the action."
–Advertising Executive
"Should be in every business library."–Executive
"Will be forming two new corporations in January using this method."–Publisher

How a *"professional"* can benefit from incorporating.

How to save from $300 to over $1,000 in the formation of the corporation alone!

What a *"foreign"* **corporation is.** A State by State list of the filing fees involved in registering a "foreign" corporation.

Learn how a corporation can sell its stock to raise capital at any time.

How a single individual can be President, Secretary and Treasurer. There is no need to have anyone involved except a single stockholder although, of course, as many as desired can be included.

How to arrange for any stock sold to an investor in a corporation to be tax deductible to the investor's personal income in the event of loss. This makes the sale of stock in a corporation far more attractive to an investor.

An outline of the many situations where an individual would benefit by incorporating.

How to legally incorporate and sell stock in a corporation without "registering" the stock.

FREE BONUS

By placing your order now, you'll receive absolutely free a copy of the Ted Nicholas best selling report, HOW & WHERE TO RAISE VENTURE CAPITAL TO FINANCE A BUSINESS. This jam packed report has a value of $6.95. 227 sources of venture capital are interested in limits of loans available from less than $100,000 to over $1,000,000 and investment policies such as long term loans.

Name, address, telephone number and individual to contact is included. Also contains complete information on how to best approach a capital source. Benefit by learning about many of the author's personal experiences.

Remember, this is yours free for ordering now — a $6.95 value. Should you decide to return corporation manual, this report is yours to keep, regardless.

Just complete coupon — immediate shipment. (Publications will be mailed individually. May arrive separately.)

TO: ENTERPRISE PUBLISHING CO., INC.
1300 Market Street, Dept.
Wilmington, Del. 19801

Please send me____copies of "HOW TO FORM YOUR OWN CORPORATION WITHOUT A LAWYER FOR UNDER $50.00" at $9.95 each, plus 45¢ postage and handling along with free bonus copy of HOW & WHERE TO RAISE VENTURE CAPITAL TO FINANCE A BUSINESS, a $6.95 value absolutely free.

☐ I prefer to have____copies of deluxe special limited Library Edition of above book, bound in cloth, gold embossing @ $12.50 each (with bonus).

It is my understanding that if I am not completely satisfied with the book after 10 days of receipt, I can return the book undamaged for a full refund.

☐ check enclosed ☐ Master Charge ☐ Carte Blanche ☐ Bank Americard ☐ Diner's Club

No.____

Signature____

NAME (Please Print)____

ADDRESS____

CITY____   STATE____   ZIP____

ADD ☐ 80¢ SP.Del.   ☐ $2.25 U.S. Air   ☐ $4.25 Fgn. Air

Mr. Nicholas has been to the White House to personally meet with the President of the United States after being selected as one of the outstanding businessmen in the Nation.   © Copyright 1975 Enterprise Publishing Co.

As advertised in the Wall Street Journal, Barrons, National Observer, New York Times, Fortune, Business Week, Nations Business , etc.

How to form your own corporation without a lawyer for under $50.⁰⁰

By Ted Nicholas

You may have considered incorporating. I'm sure you want to accomplish this in the most economical way. You may already be in business and are looking for ways to save tax dollars or limit personal liability.

You can benefit from this report if you are planning a one man business if you are associated with a partner or are the owner of a large company.

This exciting report shows you step by step how you can accomplish this for less than $50.00.

It contains tear-out forms for everything that is needed! This includes minutes, bylaws, and the actual certificate of incorporation!

It is presented in simple, clear language.

You'll learn of the many benefits of incorporating either an existing business or one that is planned.

Some of the features of the 8½ x 11, 30,000 word, 103 page report:

How you can incorporate without any capital requirement with zero capital.

The many personal tax benefits of incorporating.

How a corporation limits the personal liability for the owner(s) of a business, to the investment in the corporation. (Except for taxes)

How to actually form a corporation step by step. Included are instructions on completing the forms.

How to own and operate a corporation anonymously if desired. This assures maximum privacy.

How to form a non profit corporation. How to utilize tax "gimmicks" to personal advantage.

Find out why lawyers charge huge fees for incorporating services even when often times they prefer not to.

How a *"professional"* can benefit from incorporating.

How to save from $300 to over $1,000 in the formation of the corporation alone!

What a *"foreign"* **corporation is.** A State by State list of the filing fees involved in registering a "foreign" corporation.

Learn how a corporation can sell its stock to raise capital at any time.

How a single individual can be President, Secretary and Treasurer. There is no need to have anyone involved except a single stockholder although, of course, as many as desired can be included.

How to arrange for any stock sold to an investor in a corporation to be tax deductible to the investor's personal income in the event of loss. This makes the sale of stock in a corporation far more attractive to an investor.

An outline of the many situations where an individual would benefit by incorporating.

FLASH

Due to new tax law it is even more advantageous than ever before to incorporate. Tax rate averages only 21% for income of up to $50,000!

Sub Chapter S Corporations. What they are. How to set one up. How to operate a business as a corporation, yet be taxed on individual tax rates if more advantageous.

Learn about the many dangers and hazards of not incorporating partnerships and proprietorships.

What a Registered Agent is. How assistance is provided to individuals who incorporate. The most economical company to use. A complete section on this.

How to cut out all fees of the "middle man" normally involved in forming a corporation.

IRON CLAD GUARANTEE. If you are not completely satisfied with the book after you have it for 10 days you may return it for a full refund.

COMMENTS FROM READERS
"I want to buy several copies for my clients." - Insurance Executive
"If I'd known about this I would have incorporated years ago." -Salesman
"This report is a handy reference for me." – Lawyer
"The author is experienced in the corporate world, giving him the qualifications to write this book." Judge
"Fantastic! Do you want a partner?" Lawyer
"Good idea. Brings the concept of being incorporated within the reach of anyone." – Artist
"I was quoted a price of $1,000 each for 3 corporations I want to form! This report saves me almost $3,000!" – Business Owner
"Excellent! Written so that anyone can understand it." –Secretary
"Takes the mystery out of forming a corporation." – Printer
"Very well written. Will encourage many small businesses to incorporate." –Housewife
"Well written. Will eventually produce more business for lawyers." – Lawyer
"Great idea! I'd be glad to promote it for a piece of the action." – Advertising Executive
"Should be in every business library." –Executive
"Will be forming two new corporations in January using this method." – Publisher

States can benefit by incorporating. Also included are the steps to take after incorporating.

The reasons why ⅔rds of the corporations listed on the American and New York Stock Exchanges incorporate in Delaware—the State most friendly to corporations—and how you can have the same benefits as the largest corporations in America.

What to do if you are already incorporated in another state and want to take advantage of incorporating in Delaware, without ever visiting the State.

Learn why many "side" businesses and investments should be separately incorporated.

Just complete coupon — immediate shipment.

TO: ENTERPRISE PUBLISHING CO., INC.
      1300 Market Street, Dept.
      Wilmington, Del. 19801

Please send me____ copies of "HOW TO FORM YOUR OWN CORPORATION WITHOUT A LAWYER FOR UNDER $50.00" at $7.95 each, plus 45¢ postage and handling.

☐ I prefer to have____copies of deluxe special limited Library Edition of above book, bound in cloth, gold embossing @ $12.50 each

It is my understanding that if I am not completely satisfied with the book after 10 days of receipt, I can return the book undamaged for a full refund.

☐check enclosed ☐Master Charge ☐Carte Blanche ☐Bank Americard ☐Diner's Club

No. _____

Signature _____

NAME (Please Print) _____

ADDRESS _____

CITY _____ STATE_____ ZIP _____
ADD ☐80¢ SP.Del.   ☐$2.25 U.S. Air   ☐$4.25 Fgn. Air

Mr. Nicholas has been to the White House to personally meet with the President of the United States after being selected as one of the outstanding businessmen in the Nation.   © Copyright 1975 Enterprise Publishing Co.

Sample of variation of approach letter for P.I. sales.

Dear Mr. _____

    As a profit-making organization, I am sure you want to make full use of your facilities as much as possible.

    Throughout your programming day, the availabilities that go unsold are not making your station a cent!

    Sure, you can fill them with Public Service announcements and promos, but there must be some better way to capitalize on unsold air-time.

    Well, there is.

    A few short years ago, a new "How To" book was written by Ted Nicholas, an outstanding business consultant. The book, called HOW TO FORM YOUR OWN CORPORATION WITHOUT A LAWYER FOR UNDER $50 informs the reader how to do just that!

    As you can see from the enclosed brochure, it has been advertised in such publications as the Wall St. Journal, Fortune and The New York Times, just to name a few.

    The book is available by mail order. It sells for $7.95 plus 45¢ postage and handling and comes with a ten day money back guarantee.

    What all this means to you is profit. By advertising the book on air-time that happens to be unsold anyway, you keep $3.36 for every order you receive!

    We will also send you a 90 second spot announcement, ready for airing. If you should like more information or a sample of the book, please write or call me collect at _____.

                              Sincerely,

Sample letter to obtain editorial coverage on Newspaper's Women's pages.

As the job market shrinks and prices skyrocket, more and
more of your readers are starting their own businesses. Many women
now work out of their homes to supplement the family income. To
keep up with increased money needs, others with hobbies are expanding
them into businesses, while keeping a full time job.

Everyone has heard how all the big companies legally
save fortunes through incorporation tax savings. It is totally
legitimate, but infuriating! Although your readers could take
advantage of these same savings, most do not. Why? Because
they think incorporating is too expensive. Lawyers' charges run
as high as $1,000 -- too expensive for a home-run business.
Very often that's the entire profit.

Ted Nicholas will explain that attorneys' services are
not required by law to incorporate. Mr. Nicholas says that
incorporating any business should cost no more than $50.

More than 100,000 copies of Ted's book HOW TO FORM YOUR
OWN CORPORATION WITHOUT A LAWYER FOR UNDER $50 have been sold
for $7.95. Mr. Nicholas has been to the White House to meet with
the President of the United States, after being selected as one of
the Nation's outstanding businessmen.

Articulate, outspoken, and knowledgeable, Ted Nicholas
is ready to discuss the advantages, as well as the costs, of
incorporating. He can alert your readers to businesses they
can start with little or no capital.

In the Wall Street Journal and numerous national magazines,
people have been reading about Ted Nicholas' book, published by
Enterprise Publishing, a member of the Better Business Bureau of
Delaware. We hope you'll agree that Mr. Nicholas will make an excellent
feature for your family page since he offers a way out of difficult
family finances. Please let us know what dates are convenient for
you within the next two months. Meanwhile, please don't hesitate to
call us if we can be of help.

Sincerely,

Sample of letter for setting up School Seminar.

January ____, 1975

Dear _____:

   The latest trend in education, as you know, is toward the
practical and timely; it is a move away from the Ivory Tower and into
the real world.

   Mr. Ted Nicholas -- the internationally respected author,
business expert and lecturer -- is offering you the opportunity to
provide your interested students with a one week seminar (one hour
daily) on the broad subject of "How to Start Your Own Business."

   As you may know, Mr. Nicholas has been to the White House
to meet with the President of the United States, after being
selected as one of the Nation's outstanding businessmen.

   He would begin the Seminar -- by way of getting acquainted --
by eliciting already held business ideas of students. In the span
of one week, he would discuss the psychology of the entrepreneur,
the advantages and disadvantages of being in one's own business (the
psychology of failure), the way the free market functions, the
fundamentals of any business (production, sales, finance, research),
salesmanship and marketing, routine business ideas and problem-solving,
helpful college courses and books. He would conclude by discussing
the necessary preparation required to go into any business.

   The format is very informal; Mr. Nicholas believes
students generally learn most when they feel free to participate and
"get involved." When he has given Seminars in other public school
systems, he has proven uniquely effective in developing an "instant"
rapport with his students.

   Because of his heavy traveling schedule as well as other
commitments, Mr. Nicholas is available only until Easter.

   If you desire Ted Nicholas' Seminar at your school (which,
incidentally, he is offering at his own expense totally), please
let me know as soon as possible so arrangements can be made.

                                        Sincerely,

P.S. Because of the shrinking job market and soaring prices, providing
your students with the Nicholas Seminar would be particularly helpful
to them. (Mr. Nicholas' most recent best selling books are: WHERE
THE MONEY IS AND HOW TO GET IT and HOW TO FORM YOUR OWN CORPORATION
WITHOUT A LAWYER FOR UNDER $50.)

Sample of follow-up letter for purpose of news story.

Dear _____:

I have enjoyed our conversations regarding a story on Ted Nicholas, the well-known businessman-author. And, of course, I particularly appreciate your interest in doing something as soon as possible.

Here are some of the facts and figures in written form which you indicated were what most interested you.

As I mentioned, many of the jobless are turning to Ted Nicholas to form corporations. What is interesting to us is that Dunn & Bradstreet reported in December that the national incorporation figures for the first ten months of 1974 were off 3.1%. Meanwhile, the state of Delaware -- the home of Ted Nicholas' Company Corporation's incorporations -- has shown an increase of 22%. If we were to subtract those incorporating through Nicholas from the Delaware totals, the state of Delaware's figures would show a decline of 7.1%, even greater than the national statistic. You can see by this that Nicholas is indeed a significant part of the state of Delaware and of the national incorporation figures.

Statistically: 9,214 corporations were formed in the state of Delaware in the first ten months of 1974. With these, 2,500 were formed via Nicholas' Company Corporation. Therefore, approximately one out of every three corporations formed during that period in the state of Delaware can be attributed to Ted Nicholas.

In a relatively short period of time, HOW TO FORM YOUR OWN CORPORATION WITHOUT A LAWYER FOR UNDER $50 has sold in excess of 100,000 copies at $7.95 in soft cover and $12.95 in hard cover. Additionally, Mr. Nicholas has now incorporated thousands of clients from all fifty states and several foreign countries.

In spite of the unofficial groans of the Bar Association when Mr. Nicholas' book first appeared -- many lawyers are now using Nicholas' book to expedite their own private practices.

Additionally, Mr Nicholas (who is without any of the normal teaching credentials) was invited to conduct a special Seminar in the Wilmington Public School System on the subject of "How to Start Your Own Business." The course is now being repeated due to the popular demand generated by students.

Page #2.

        Per our last phone conversation, I will be giving you a
call in a few days to see if we can set a date for you to meet with
Mr. Nicholas. If I can be of any assistance in the meantime, please
do not hesitate to call.

                                Cordially,

Sample
Sales Information for Book Dealers

SALES INFORMATION

HOW TO FORM YOUR OWN CORPORATION WITHOUT A LAWYER
UNDER $50

by Ted Nicholas

Included is information on other publications by
Enterprise Publishing Company
1300 Market Street
Wilmington, Delaware 19801

We assume you have read and benefited personally from the remarkable book HOW TO FORM YOUR OWN CORPORATION WITHOUT A LAWYER FOR UNDER $50 by Ted Nicholas.

The following will detail the market on a number of proven sales methods. You will make steady and continuing profits by applying your skills to the sale of this book. Not only will you make money, but you will have the pleasure of knowing that your customers will save money and obtain immediate protection and benefits. You will also be strengthening our Free Enterprise system. We don't know a better way of doing that than by encouraging the foundation of corporations. They are the backbone of our economic system and way of life.

Our nationwide advertising has created a built-in demand for the book. Most experts say that for every book bought by mail order, two people seek the book in a bookstore or elsewhere. This is where you come into the marketing picture.

Over 200 full page ads have run in publications such as: Newsweek, Time, Salesman's Opportunity, Nation's Business, Specialty Salesman, U.S. News & World Report, Signature, Barrons, Money, Carte Blanche, American Scientist, Human Events, Capitalist Reporter, Money Making Opportunities, Holiday Inn, Business Week, Wall Street Journal, Esquire, Forbes, New York Times, etc.

In 1974 the advertising budget for this single title was in excess of $300,000! To our knowledge this is the largest advertising budget for any book ever published.

In 1975 plans are at least equal to that advertising budget. Our goal is to sell several hundred thousand copies. We would like you to join us and share in the profit. Best of all, each year there is a continuing large market. Every time someone goes into business or plans to, he or she is a prospect. This feature assures continuing sales year after year.

THE MARKET

At the present time there are approximately 15 million un-incorporated business owners in the U.S. Virtually all of these individuals would benefit by having a copy of this book. Prior to the publication of this book over 300,000 people in the U.S. incor-porated each year. The corporation manual is adding thousands more. The different types of individuals and situations that are prospects for the book include:

1. Every owner of a business.

2. The large corporation that wishes to form subsidiary corporations at low cost. (This makes stockholders very happy and saves time on the part of lawyers. A secretary can complete the forms in the book in minutes!)

3. The homeowner who operates a part-time business out of his home.

When introducing this book to your prospect, you can of course, sell it outright at the suggested retail price of $7.95, or leave it with the individual on approval for ten days when you come back to pick up your check. You will find that both methods are effective. It has always been our policy to sell with an absolute money back guarantee. Experience has shown that we have a 1% return rate which is insignificant.

There are several additional sales outlets that have proven to be outstanding book sales, those are:

1. Bookstores - some already stock the book. You are encouraged to sell to the ones that do not. The book makes a fine permanent addition to the business or reference section of any bookstore.

2. Newsstands.

3. Gift shops.

4. Business stationers and supply stores.

5. Libraries, including public, high school, technical and business. These outlets are surprisingly good for repeat sales. Either the book gets used so often that it is replaced or people tear out the forms causing a reorder.

6. Conventions, exhibits and trade shows. Books can be sold in large quantity right on the spot from a booth. You can lease a booth or space in one.

7. Organizations that are interested in raising money through their membership. (Here a large volume of copies can be sold.) Also, volume sales can be obtained if you deliver a talk to the organization and have copies available there for the members. (You can use this information and the book as a guide to prepare the talk.)

A suggested discount schedule for these outlets is as follows:

WHOLESALE PRICE AND DISCOUNT SCHEDULE

HOW TO FORM YOUR OWN CORPORATION WITHOUT A LAWYER FOR UNDER $50

by Ted Nicholas

Bookstores	Retail Price	Discount	Price Per Book
1-2 copies	$ 7.95	20%	$ 6.35 (plus 23¢ shipping)
3-9 copies	$ 7.95	30%	$ 5.55 postpaid
10 & over	$ 7.95	40%	$ 4.75 postpaid
Libraries	$ 7.95	No Discount	$ 7.95
Special Deluxe Edition	$12.50	No Discount	$12.50

DIRECT MAIL

This book has proven successful in direct mail. If you are in the mail order business, the book sells. The buyer is the business owner or opportunity seeker. Enclosed is a brochure that you may reproduce with your name and return address on it. Also, if you are in the direct mail business or ship mail orders to customers for other products, you will find that enclosing the offer with others is also successful.

DISPLAY ADS

We enclose sample display advertising that has demonstrated its success. Consumer magazines as well as the trade journals that serve business and industry are productive. With the many magazines, newspapers and trade journals that exist in the country, in spite of our own nationwide advertising efforts, there is no possible way that we can cover the entire market. If it is your desire to run this kind of advertising, you may use the enclosed copy, having orders go directly to you.

We suggest you test on a small scale to prove that the particular market you select is profitable before expanding to larger circulation.

CLASSIFIED ADVERTISING

Classified advertising on behalf of the book has also proven useful. This is a low cost way to generate exposure and interest in the book. You may utilize the following tested classified advertising copy and run it in whatever publication you wish. Of course, the mailing address for orders would be yours. We have found that a street address works better than a post office box. The categories under which the advertising has proven productive are Business Services or Business Opportunities.

SAMPLE OF CLASSIFIED ADVERTISING

HOW TO FORM YOUR OWN CORPORATION WITHOUT A LAWYER FOR UNDER $50
by Ted Nicholas

Hundreds of money and tax saving ideas. Free details.
Enterprise Publishing Co.
1300 Market Street   (substitute your address)
Wilmington, DE 19801

In summary, we have briefly outlined the various ways that you can sell this outstanding book. The market is vast and ever changing and ever growing each year. It is our objective, with your sales skills, to further penetrate this multi-million person market, for we will both profit. If you have any questions at any time, do not hesitate to drop us a line.

TOP SELLING PUBLICATIONS FROM ENTERPRISE PUBLISHING CO., INC.

1. **HOW TO FORM YOUR OWN CORPORATION WITHOUT A LAWYER FOR UNDER $50.00**
Complete with tear-out forms. Contains numerous money and tax saving ideas. Now in its second big printing. Rapidly becoming a best seller.

by **Ted Nicholas**
$7.95
Plus 45¢ postage and handling.
$12.50
Plus 45¢ postage and handling.

1A. Beautifully bound edition for your business library. Ideal for gifts.

2. **HOW AND WHERE TO RAISE VENTURE CAPITAL TO FINANCE A BUSINESS**
227 sources of venture capital, classified by name, address, telephone number and individual to contact. Also includes information as to how to approach a capital source, and many of the author's personal experiences.

by **Ted Nicholas**
$6.95 Postpaid
Printed in the form of a report.

3. **WHERE THE MONEY IS AND HOW TO GET IT**
How and where to raise capital for a business. Contains hundreds of sources of loans and venture capital. Includes names, addresses and phone numbers. Fully expanded list includes venture capital firms, state sources, and selected banks. Techniques save you time and produce results. A must for every business library.

by **Ted Nicholas**
$10.00 Clothbound
Plus 45¢ postage and handling.
Publication Date: August 1973

4. **HOW TO SET UP YOUR OWN MEDICAL REIMBURSEMENT PLAN**
Report shows how all medical and dental expenses are fully tax deductible. This includes prescription drugs and applies to a business owner and his family. Contains a blank form with instructions for completion. Can be made effective immediately. This eye opening report takes only a few minutes to read. This valuable tax angle is used by businessmen, small and large, throughout the nation. It has saved people thousands of dollars in taxes. Weeks of research condensed in a few pages.

by **Ted Nicholas**
$5.00 Postpaid
Printed in the form of a report.

All publications sold with a 10 day money back guarantee

DEALER DISCOUNT SCHEDULE

12   1 Dozen - 40%

72   6 Dozen - 45%

144 1 Gross - 50%

12×12

Same discount schedule applies for other Enterprise Publishing Co. publications. Orders may be combined to obtain quantity discounts.

Note: On your first dealer order, be sure to deduct $7.95 from your check for your original purchase.

O R D E R   F O R M

FROM: _____

_____

_____

TO: ENTERPRISE PUBLISHING COMPANY
      1300 Market Street
      Wilmington, Delaware 19801

QUANTITY   TITLE   PRICE

_____   _____ $_____

_____   _____ $_____

_____   _____ $_____

_____   _____ $_____

Enclosed is a Check _____ Money Order _____

NOTE: We pay shipping charges on all orders.

ENTERPRISE PUBLISHING CO.   1000 OAKFIELD LANE/WILMINGTON, DELAWARE 19810

```
* * * * * * * * * * * * * * * * * * * * * * * * * * * * * * * * *
*                                                               *
*                     A Special Invitation                      *
*                                                               *
*  To YOU As A Present Or Future Business Owner Who Wishes To    *
*  Enjoy The Tax Savings, Limited Personal Liability And The    *
*  Many Other Benefits Of INCORPORATING Your Business...        *
*                                                               *
*      We Will Send You The PROVEN, Best-Selling Book:          *
*                                                               *
*  " H O W  T O  F O R M  Y O U R  O W N  C O R P O R A T I O N *
*                                                               *
*     W I T H O U T  A  L A W Y E R  F O R  U N D E R  $ 5 0 "  *
*                                                               *
*  (Especially Valuable In Today's Regulation-Controlled Economy*
*  That Gives Corporations SPECIAL BENEFITS Which Individual    *
*  Business Owners, Like Yourself, Do Not Enjoy!)               *
*                                                               *
*     * TO EVALUATE FOR 10 DAYS AT OUR RISK, NOT YOURS,         *
*       UNDER OUR IRONCLAD REFUND GUARANTEE!                    *
*                                                               *
*     * PLUS...A $5.00 SPECIAL REPORT, "HOW TO SET UP           *
*       YOUR OWN MEDICAL REIMBURSEMENT PLAN"...YOURS TO         *
*       KEEP, EVEN IF YOU RETURN THIS VALUABLE BOOK!            *
*                                                               *
* * * * * * * * * * * * * * * * * * * * * * * * * * * * * * * * *
```

The Founder of 18 Successful Corporations
Tells You How To Form Your OWN Corporation
-- AND SAVE $200 TO $1,000 IN LEGAL FEES!

Thousands and thousands of corporations have already been formed by the
more than 75,000 readers of this proven, practical guide. These individuals live in every one of the 50 states and in countries around the
world.

Lawyers' fees for incorporating range from $200 to $1,000 and more. But
a little-known fact is that in many states an individual can legally
incorporate without the services of a lawyer.

In addition to initial legal fees, the businessmen who have followed the
valuable advice in this book are now saving thousands of dollars in taxes
and personal liability claims...putting more money into their own pockets
and enjoying the many fringe benefits and other special advantages of
their own corporation.

(And this invaluable book, "HOW TO FORM YOUR OWN CORPORATION
WITHOUT A LAWYER FOR UNDER $50", shows you, too, how to do it!
Everything you need to form your own corporation is included.)

The author, Ted Nicholas, knows what he's talking about. Starting with
only $800, he formed his first corporation when he was still in his early
twenty's. Since then, he has formed 17 more corporations, sold and merged
some, and today he is a successful businessman still operating 3 of his
own corporations!

And now Ted Nicholas wants to share his proven methods with YOU...

Mr. Nicholas learned how to start his corporations the hard way...the expensive way...by experience. There were no books available like this one. He, like most of us, has had his share of failures as well as successes. And he learned from both.

Now you can avoid the costly mistakes Ted Nicholas made...and take advantage of the money-saving, profit-making corporation-forming techniques he discovered.

Note! →

And right now, "HOW TO FORM YOUR OWN CORPORATION WITHOUT A LAWYER FOR UNDER $50" can be especially valuable to you as the present or future owner of a small business, a partner in a business or the owner of a large company.

Because in these days of high personal income taxes and other economic problems, the many special tax-shelter benefits and other timely advantages of a corporation are more attractive than ever before!

So right now is the opportune time to join the more than 75,000 other alert business-minded individuals who have benefited from Mr. Nicholas's sound, sensible and proven corporation-forming techniques by accepting this advantageous special offer...

"HOW TO FORM A CORPORATION WITHOUT A LAWYER FOR UNDER $50" is yours to evaluate for 10 days under our ironclad refund guarantee. You take absolutely no risk. If you are not completely satisfied with this truly unique and helpful book, you may return it undamaged within 10 days after receiving it for a full, no-questions-asked refund.

And as an extra bonus for accepting this offer now, you will also receive the $5.00 Special Report, "HOW TO SET UP YOUR OWN MEDICAL REIMBURSEMENT PLAN". This Report shows you how to make the Plan effective immediately and save hundreds of dollars that may be now going down the drain in taxes.

You can even charge the book on your credit card, or send along your check for only $7.95 plus postage...and it's tax-deductible.

In either case, by mailing the enclosed Special Request Card in the postage-paid envelope today, you can soon start to enjoy the savings and benefits of your own corporation.

Sincerely yours,

Dale Palmer

Dale Palmer
Assistant to the President

DP/sr

HOW TO FORM YOUR OWN CORPORATION WITHOUT A LAWYER FOR UNDER $50

This book is for you — if you have ever considered incorporating your present or future business or professional practice but were stopped by the complications and high fees you thought had to be involved.

The ADVANTAGES of the corporate form of business or professional organization far outweigh the disadvantages. Among the advantages are:

- Limited personal liability
- Ease of raising capital
- Tax savings
- Continuity of life
- Ease of transferability of ownership
- Separate legal being

How To Form Your Own Corporation Without A Lawyer For Under $50 was written by Ted Nicholas — a successful business consultant. You, too, can benefit from this proven book — now in its 5th big printing — if you are planning a one-man business, if you want to convert a partnership, or are the owner of a large firm, or are a professional person.

It's all here . . . how to do it for under $50 . . . in this easy-to-follow, step-by-step guide.

HERE ARE THE HIGHLIGHTS OF THIS AMAZING BOOK:

How you can incorporate without any capital requirement.

The many personal tax benefits of incorporating.

How a corporation limits the personal liability for the owner(s) of a business to the investment in the corporation. (Except for taxes.)

How to actually form a corporation step-by-step. Included are instructions on completing the forms.

How to own and operate a corporation anonymously if desired. This assures maximum privacy.

How to form a non-profit corporation. How to utilize tax "gimmicks" to personal advantage.

Find out why lawyers charge huge fees for incorporating services even when often-times they prefer not to.

How a "professional" can benefit from incorporating.

Learn how and why you can legally incorporate without the services of a lawyer. It is a fallacy that, as most people believe, it is necessary to have a lawyer to incorporate.

How to form an "open" or "close" corporation and the difference between them. **Report contains tear-out forms.**

Sub Chapter S Corporations. What they are. How to set one up. How to operate a business as a corporation, yet be taxed on individual tax rates — if more advantageous.

Learn about the many dangers and hazards of NOT incorporating partnerships and proprietorships.

What a Registered Agent is. How assistance is provided to individuals who incorporate. The most economical company to use. A complete section on this.

How to cut out ALL fees of the "middle man" normally involved in forming a corporation.

How to save from $200 to over $1,000 in the formation of the corporation alone.

What a "foreign" corporation is. A state-by-state list of filing fees involved in registering a "foreign" corporation.

Learn how a corporation can sell its stock to raise capital at any time.

How a single individual can hold ALL offices in a corporation. There is no need to have anyone involved except a single stockholder although, of course, as many as desired can be included.

How to arrange for any stock sold to an investor in a corporation to be tax deductible to the investor's personal income in the event of loss. This makes the sale of stock in a corporation far more attractive to an investor.

An outline of the many situations where an individual would benefit by incorporation.

How to legally incorporate and sell stock in a corporation *without "registering"* the stock.

What par and no par value stock are and which is the most practical.

How an existing, unincorporated business anywhere in the United States **can benefit by incorporating.** Also included are the steps to take after incorporating.

The reasons why most of the corporations listed on the American and New York Stock Exchanges **incorporate in Delaware** — the state most friendly to corporations — and **how YOU can have the SAME benefits** as the largest corporations in America.

What to do if you are already incorporated in another state and want to take advantage of incorporating in Delaware.

Learn why many PART-TIME businesses and investments should be separately incorporated.

A FEW WORDS ABOUT THE SUCCESSFUL INCORPORATOR —AUTHOR

Ted Nicholas, 39-year old businessman-author, has been in his own business since he was 22. During his business career he has founded 18 corporations in diverse businesses, including food, confectionery, real estate, machinery and licensing. All were small businesses. He has experienced success and failure and often states that he has learned more from failure than from success.

Having gained first-hand experience in the business world, Mr. Nicholas decided there was a need for a BOOK ON INCORPORATING, directed toward the small businessman who could not afford high legal fees. *The motivating factor behind his book is his strong belief in the concept that the individual businessman should have available to him the knowledge and benefits heretofore available only to the largest corporations in America.*

Mr. Nicholas has appeared on radio and television, been a guest speaker before various groups, and not too long ago, he was selected as one of the outstanding young businessmen in the nation and was invited to meet with Lyndon B. Johnson, the President of the United States.

IRONCLAD REFUND GUARANTEE

If you are not entirely satisfied with **How To Form Your Own Corporation Without A Lawyer For Under $50** you may return it undamaged within 10 days of receipt for a full refund. No questions asked and you may *keep* your bonus copy of "How To Set Up Your Own Medical Reimbursement Plan."

SPECIAL $5.00 BONUS REPORT INCLUDED

HOW TO SET UP YOUR OWN MEDICAL REIMBURSEMENT PLAN

A specially-researched and written Report that shows you how ALL medical and dental expenses are fully deductible, even including prescription drugs. This applies not only to the business owner but to his family as well. The Report contains a blank form with simple-to-follow instructions for completion. This practical PLAN can be made effective immediately.

"How To Set Up Your Own Medical Reimbursement Plan" is an eye-opening Report that only takes a few minutes to read. These valuable, proven tax-saving tips are now used by businessmen, small and large, throughout the nation. The $5 they spent for this Report has saved them thousands of dollars in taxes. It can do the same for you. And it is yours as a BONUS.

SPECIAL GUARANTEED OFFER

Start right away to enjoy the savings and benefits of incorporating by requesting your personal no-risk evaluation copy of **HOW TO FORM YOUR OWN CORPORATION WITHOUT A LAWYER FOR UNDER $50** . . . today. Charge it to your credit card or send your check for $7.95 plus postage. And you will also receive a copy of "How to Set Up Your Own Medical Reimbursement Plan" at no additional cost . . . yours to keep free, in any case. In today's "regulated" business economy offering more-profitable-than-ever reasons for forming your own corporation, you couldn't pick a better time to mail the Request Card in the postage-paid envelope than right *now!*

A Few of the Enthusiastic "Thank-Yous" from People Who Have Incorporated by Using This Book.

"IT OPENS TO THE 'LITTLE GUY' A WHOLE NEW DIMENSION OF BUSINESS"
"The book is excellent, clear, concise and enlightening. It opens to the 'little guy' in business a whole new dimension of business opportunities. Thank you for making it available.

Stu Sinclair, President, CWCA Inc., Ohio

"HELPS CREATE A CORPORATION WITHOUT EXTREMELY HIGH LEGAL FEES"
"The service offered by your company helps one create a corporation without the extremely high legal fees involved in hiring an attorney."

President, Torch Inc., North Carolina

"MORE HELPFUL IN OUR RECENT INCORPORATION THAN ANY OTHER SOURCE"
"Your book was more help in our recent incorporation than any other single source. We would recommend it highly to anyone wishing to incroporate.

Allyn T. Gallant, President A. T. Gallant & Co. Inc., Calif.

"EXCELLENT"
"Excellent — The only way — I recommend it for all up-and-coming capitalists.

Roger C. Brown, President, RCB International Inc., Kentucky

"SAVED ME CONSIDERABLE EXPENSE"
"Excellent, concise, and highly informative. Saved me considerable expense and time."

Curtis S. Jenkins, President, NATCO Int'l Corp., Colorado

"VERY HELPFUL"
"Mr. Nicholas' book was satisfactory and very helpful and complete in every way."

Les Tiller, President, American Enterprises, Inc., Illinois

"A BOON TO THE PERSON WHO WISHES TO INCORPORATE"
"Mr. Nicholas' book is a boon to the small business person who wishes to incorporate. It is simple to follow and the savings in fees and costs are tremendous."

Nancy Y. Zepernick, President, NYZ Enterprises, Inc., Va.

"INVALUABLE"
"Mr. Nicholas' book is invaluable to anyone desiring to establish himself in the corporation world. The professionalism of your organization is worth much to any individual or commercial organization.

Gordon M. Towns, President, A.U.L.L. Inc., Arkansas

"WORTH MANY TIMES PURCHASE PRICE"
"Reread important parts again . . . worth many times purchase price."

J. J. Sunbury, Pennsylvania

"WE INTEND TO INCORPORATE"
"Your book was excellent! We intend to incorporate within the next few days."

C. B. Lindhurst, N.Y.

"UNDER-PRICED . . WE'D SPENT 50 TIMES THAT AMOUNT"
"Mr. Nicholas' book is the most under-priced anywhere. Prior to obtaining a copy we'd spent 50 times that amount with disappointing results."

Howard Jacobs, President, Omnitron Inc., Canada

REVIEWERS' ENTHUSIASTIC COMMENTS

SAN FRANCISCO CHRONICLE
"Handy book . . . Describes in laymen's terms how to proceed . . . Old American spirit lives."

NEW ENGLAND BUSINESS JOURNAL
"Tells how to incorporate . . . without capital . . . limits personal liability."

SACRAMENTO BEE
"Anyone thinking of incorporating . . . should not skip any pages."

BOOK ENDS N' ODDS
"My attorney, Ralph Benson, is boosting book."

LOS ANGELES HERALD EXAMINER
"Step-by-step instructional manual."

DELAWARE TODAY
"One attorney who read it said he'd like his secretary to use it for quick reference."

HOME OFFICE REPORT
"Even for a one-man business with little or no capital."

CORPORATE FINANCE NEWSLETTER
"For those tired of paying what can amount to thousands in legal fees. One of the best 'HOW TO' books we have seen."

ENTERPRISE PUBLISHING CO.
1000 OAKFIELD LANE
WILMINGTON, DELAWARE 19810

Samples of Book Reviews and News Stories

DELAWARE TODAY DECEMBER 1973

BOOKS

HOW TO FORM YOUR OWN COR-
PORATION WITHOUT A LAWYER
FOR UNDER $50 by Ted Nicholas,
103 pages. Published by Enterprise Pub-
lishing, Wilmington, Del., $7.95.

The author of this handy-dandy how-to-do-it volume has got to be a super promoter. The first thought occuring to one upon seeing it is: "Why didn't somebody think of this before?"

It couldn't have been too difficult to put together; the printing is adequate but far from imaginative; and it does sell for the substantial sum of $7.95 (plus 45 cents postage and handling).

The book docs what it says it does — tells you how to form a corporation yourself for under $50 ($46.50 to be exact). But it does something more too: it promotes the author's corporation service company.

In fact, if there is a basic fault with the volume, it's the attempt to push you onto the corporate path. If you engaged an attorney — and granted you would be spending a minimum of $200 and probably more by the time you were through — you would receive advice and counsel on whether you should in fact form a corporation, or whether some other vehicle such as a sole proprietorship would be more advantageous from, for example, a tax standpoint.

But the Nicholas book quickly disposes of other routes. You get the disadvantages of forming an individual proprietorship or a partnership and the advantages of forming a corporation. You don't adequately get the advantages of the proprietorship or partnership approaches nor the disadvantages of incorporating.

Nicholas pushes his own company — Corporation Company, Inc. — hard. Whereas other corporation service companies receive a mention in a small-print listing, the Nicholas company receives its own chapter (well, it's his book, right?) and is presented as the salvation of the little man. It may be, but one has to be suspicious when something is presented in such a one-sided way.

The book does contain useful information, and one attorney who read it said he'd like his secretary to keep a copy on her desk for quick reference. Besides learning how to form your corporation — even the necessary forms are included, along with bylaws, corporate meeting minutes, etc. — you get useful information on Delaware corporations qualifying in other states on a state-by-state basis. Other chapters tell you such things as how to operate anonymously or how to become a "Subchapter S", non-profit, or professional corporation.

Delaware corporation laws are deliberately simple, and thus the book is easy to read and to follow.

Actually, it probably will cost you more than the $50 to follow this system since the $46.50 doesn't include a corporate seal, which you need and can run between $5 and $10. If you want one of those corporation kits, that will be another $20 or more. But that's quibbling. The method is much less expensive than an attorney.

It comes down to this: should you save the initial money and probably be all right, or should you spend more and have the security of knowing you've received more expert and individualized attention. If you choose the former path, HOW TO FORM YOUR OWN CORPORATION WITHOUT A LAWYER FOR UNDER $50 might be for you.

To get a copy, send a check for $7.95 plus 45 cents for postage and handling to Enterprise Publishing Co., Inc., 1000 Oakfield Lane, Wilmington, Del. 19810.

By KEITH MOORE

High school students are being asked to consider starting their own businesses as an alternative to looking for a job at a time when the prospects for finding employment are not good.

That small minority of high school graduates who do not go on to college are being advised by an exprt ein the field just how to go about setting up a business or how to approach companies with an idea for imprving already existing Ted Nicholas, a businessman who has had some measure of success in encouraging students in schools outside the city to make the move, addressed four high school classes last week adn will address one tomorrow. He said many of the students were already thinking along the lines of setting up their own businesses, but "they didn't know where to start."

Lots of Good Idleas

In one talk to a class of about 35 students at Canarsie High School, Nicholas said he heard any number of "viable" ideas that ranged from setting up a record store to organizing a cosmetic manufacturing business.

But he said that so much of the students' training was geared toward applying for and getting a job that "They never really gave very serious thought to their ideas for starting a business."

Asked if his seminars included tips on the possible pitfalls of business, Nicholas said some of the students were already aware of them and that the drawbacks had inhibiited them "from taking the first step." But he added that the advantages outweighed the disadvantages.

As a result of similar seminars in Delaware, one student set up his own roofing business while still in school, accroding to Nicholas. Another student opened a retail store, Nicholas said.

Seeing the Opportunity

The emphasis, Nicholas said was not on large businesses at first. "You have to start small," he said, "but as long as these kids know that there is an opportunity out there that is worth exploring, that's the important thing."

The students were impressed, said Larry Solomon, a teacher at Canarsie, "I can stand up here in front of the class and talk all I want to, but they were impressed because this was a successful businessman talking," Solomon said.

"The only problem," one student said, was that the talk was too short.

"But at least he didn't try to give us a snow job," added another student.

* * *

HIGH SCHOOL NOTEBOOK

SUNDAY NEWS
NEW YORK'S PICTURE NEWSPAPER

LOCAL NEWS AND FEATURES
HOME IMPROVEMENT
YOI SUNDAY NEWS, MARCH 16, 1975 ● B76
WORLD OF ANIMALS
CLASSIFIED

LIVING in Queens 2

CAPITALIST REPORTER
Vol. 5 No.2

March/April, 1975

The king

If there is a king in the do-it yourself law arena, it is Ted Nicholas, the shrewd, savvy author of *How To Form Your Own Corporation Without A Lawyer For Under $50.00.* The book has turned into a three-way money-maker for Nicholas.

The volume is published by Nicholas' Enterprise Publishing Co., Inc. (sales—approximately $750,000 per year). It is heavily promoted by Nicholas' own advertising company called the Peterson Advertising Agency. Futhermore, the book includes a not-too-subtle pitch urging users who do incorporate per the book's suggestions (i.e., in Delaware) to use as their legally required mailing address the services of Nicholas' third company, the Company Corporation (sales—approximately $100,000 per year).

By his own account, the 39-year-old Nicholas (real name, Ted Nicholas Peterson) picked up his expertise during his seventeen years of business experience. During that period, he started some eighteen different companies: some of them successes; some of them failures; many of them incorporated.

It was the frequent process of incorporation that gradually opened Nicholas' eyes to the fact that the procedure was a very simple one, performed more often by his attorney's competent legal secretary than his (high-priced) attorney. Thus, the idea for the book was born.

The title of Nicholas' book is slightly misleading. The incorporation fee, per se, is less than $50. But if the incorporator should have the bad fortune of living in California, for example, he would be forced to pay an additional $557 to cover fees of a corporation "foreign" to that state. Fees such as this apply in every state, and Nicholas' book includes a table properly detailing all fees. (For the record, the cheapest state is Wyoming, which charges a total of $10.00 for its Certificate of Authority.)

The book explains the three forms of ownership (corporate, individual proprietorship and partnership) and lists their lawyer-created advantages and disadvantages in terms of legal liabilities and tax rates. Those who decide they are best off incorporating are urged to do so in Delaware.

Nicholas' book has probably been the cause of an upsurge of incorporations in the past year because, for the first time, it became possible for the layman to obtain some clear-cut understanding of the advantages and disadvantages of incorporating without a cloud of obfuscating legalese. Or its expense. Nicholas admits to being surprised by the kind of person attracted to his book. "They're more sophisticated than I thought they would be. Professional people like doctors and engineers. And the wheeler-dealer types."

Nicholas is quick to credit Dacey's legal triumph for his labor—undisturbed by any of the state bar associations or the national bar association—in selling and promoting his legal self-help manual. Still, the Delaware Bar Association has been lukewarm in its enthusiasm for the book. The full membership voted to take no action against it, even though there was a division of opinion in the unauthorized practice committee as to whether or not it constituted an unauthorized practice of law.

But if the Bar Association had issued an injunction against the book, Ted Nicholas feels that it would be very short-sighted on their part.

"The more corporations that form in Delaware, the more legal work will come to the state," he says. And as for the out-of-state grumblings from other bar associations whose membership is losing incorporation business, Nicholas points out that, as these businesses are encouraged to grow and prosper, there will be even more need for lawyers (as businessmen enter into contracts, go public, etc.). What money the lawyers are losing on the incorporation procedure, they'll more than make up with the new corporations' legal business.

The book sells for $7.95 (include 45¢ for postage) and is available from:

Enterprise Publishing Co., Inc.
1000 Oakfield Land Dept.4X
Wilmington, Del. 19810

by NONA AGUILAR

DO-IT-YOURSELF LAW
Part 2: CIVIL LAW

SUNDAY NEWS

NEW YORK'S PICTURE NEWSPAPER ®

★★★★
FINAL

30¢

Vol. 54. No. 46   Copr. 1975 New York News Inc.   New York, N.Y. 10017, Sunday, March 16, 1975★   Sunny, 30-47. Details p. 157

Start Your Own Biz for Money & Fun, Students Told

By JOHN HENRY

Though many believe the economy is in the worst shape it has been in since the Depression, a businessman/author from Wilmington. Del, last week was advising high school students here that now may be the time to "start your own business."

If anything, said Ted Nicholas, who has started some 20 companies and written two books on entrepeneurship, the current recession underscores the attractiveness of being your own boss.

"Right now there are over 100,000 GM workers laid off," he told a class of about 50 seniors at the William Howard Taft High School in the Bronx the other day. "Every one of them thought they were secure. They had bought the cultural mythology.

"There isn't a company on earth that can guarantee you anything."

Nicholas, who was invited by the city's Board of Education to share his views free of charge with students at five high schools here, admits that people who start their own businesses also risk failing as he himself did—twice.

("I lost everything I had," the 41-year-old self-made entrepeneur recalled of those reverses.) But he left the unmistakable impression that the potential rewards of being one's own boss outweigh the potential risks.

"The only place you can make a lot of money is in your own business," said Nicholas, who describes his own net worth as being "in seven figures." He added, "it's a lot more fun owning your own business."

Unfortunately, he told the students, the nation's education system teaches "you how to be a member of a group," not how to become a self-starter. But the biggest deterrent to starting a business, he asserted, is the belief, pervasive in American society, that "to fail in anything is a horrible thing."

According to Nicholas, most failures occur not because a business concept isn't sound but because the entrepeneur hasn't planned his or her venture carefully enough.

To illustrate the preparation necessary to launch a business, he led one student who wanted to run a women's clothing boutique through the steps that would be required to start such a shop.

When the subject of money arose, he said to some laughter, "Suppose the cost is $15,000, but between us we have 15 cents." He then explained that even this seemingly insurmountable obstacle could be overcome if a large number of the student's acquaintances could be persuaded to invest money in the venture in return for stock in it.

"A lot of businesses you can start with zero capital," he said, citing a typing school as an example.

He said that, if strapped for funds, one could start such an enterprise in his or her own home—"assuming it's big enough,"—with leased typewriters. If leasing isn't possible, "you can start with one typewriter—your own," he advised.

Though he himself attended college, he doesn't think a bachelors degree is a prerequisite to becoming a self-made capitalist. Said Nicholas, "Five thousand new millionaires will be made this year and a great many won't have gone to college." Some students who do attend college would have been better prepared for running a business if they had gone to vocational school instead, he told an interviewer.

He said some students near Wilmington had started profitable firms in fields ranging from roofing to photography while still in high school and suggested that such businesses were one way to develop entrepeneurial skills at an early age.

Another way, he said, was the more traditional one of getting experience with an existing firm before leaving it to start one's own concern in the same field. He advised students to get such experience even if it meant their working at the outset for an employer without pay for a week or even a month as he once did—a suggestion that raised some eyebrows.

Nicholas, one of whose books is entitled "How to Form Your Own Corporation Without a Lawyer for Under $50," says he got interested in lecturing to students when the high school that two of his children attended asked him to speak on entrepeneurship.

He says he enjoys his contact with high school students because they give him ideas he can incorporate in a school he hopes to establish which would teach people how to start their own businesses.

Such a school is needed, he said because even some of the nation's most prestigious graduate business schools teach students merely "how to be someone else's employe."

"The Service Designed To Be Better"

THE PROFESSIONAL INVESTOR®

- 142 -

LYNATRACE, INC.   P. O. BOX 2144   POMPANO BEACH, FLORIDA 33061

| Volume No. 4, Issue No. 20 | REGISTERED WITH S.E.C. AS AN INVESTMENT ADVISER | Friday, September 27, 1974 |

A PASS ALONG

We saw an interesting item in THE COMPANY CORPORATION NEWSLETTER. We reprint it in its entirety.

"Another Reason to Incorporate –

We recently attended a meeting of the Federal Bar Association. An interesting idea was presented which we would like to pass along.

Many people find themselves near 65 and self-employed. If this business is not incorporated all income derived by the proprietor is, of course taxable income to him. If his income is higher than $2,400 per year he would lose his social security benefits which begin at age 65. If a person in those circumstances incorporates his business, salaries can be paid to other employees of the business, i.e. family members. Then the owner or majority shareholder of the business who was formerly a proprietor can either draw a lesser salary so that he does not lose his social security benefits or, in fact, have all the profits of the business go to other family member employees. The effect on the proprietor is such that it often is advantageous to incorporate under the above circumstances."

Sounds good, but we sure as heck suggest you consult your attorney, tax adviser, or someone definitely in the know before you commit yourself.

The company that published the above naturally favors additional incorporations because they publish a book telling you how to do your own incorporations, and also acts as agents for Corporations formed in Delaware.

And while we can't vouch for the tax ploy reprinted above, we can give an unqualified endorsement to the little book this company sells. We bought it a year ago, and have since formed two corporations ourself with about 10 minutes effort apiece, and at a cost of $94 and change for each one. The only possible gripe we can offer, is that the title is a little misleading. While technically possible if you have a bona fide address in Delaware and want to print your own Corporate kit, the actual cost as we said is more like $94. The title: "How To Form Your Own Corporation Without A Lawyer For Under $50." May be obtained from Enterprise Publishing Co., 1000 Oakfield Lane, Dept., Wilmington, Delaware 19810. $10.40 includes postage and handling.

Before all you attorneys among our subscribers write and denounce us, just stop and think of all the new, profitable legal work that is created by the formation of new corporations. Even the smallest corporation needs the service of a lawyer a couple of times a year. Give us a break, when we're starting-up, we don't have the $500 to spare; later on – you'll get yours; it never fails!

SAN DIEGO UNION

December, 1973

TED NICHOLAS
... Author here

Corporate Guideline Offered

Author Ted Nicholas of Wilmington, Del., has been in San Diego in recent days to promote two books — one in its fourth printing and another coming out next year.

The older book, "How to Form Your Own Corporation without a Lawyer for under $50," tells businessmen how to incorporate in every state, but particularly Delaware, where two-thirds of New York and American Stock Exchange companies incorporate.

Many readers can incorporate by simply tearing out perforated forms in the book and mailing them to appropriate authorities.

"Lawyers charge anywhere from $500 to $3,000 for such service," Nicholas said in an interview. "This book is for the company with $1,000 to $10 million in sales. A number of millionaires are buying it."

Nicholas will profit doubly from the book. As well as getting a portion of total sales, his company, The Corporation Co., Inc., in Wilmington, provides a mailing address and mail service for companies which incorporate in Delaware but are headquartered far away.

Nicholas' company has 1,050 clients who pay $25 a year for the Delaware address and mailing services. Another 30 companies in Delaware provide the same service, Nicholas said.

Nicholas' other book, "Where the Money Is and How to Get It," is a nuts-and-bolts how-to-do-it on getting venture capital to back an enterprise. Much of the book is taken up by long lists of companies, foundations and institutions who have money available for inventors, entrepreneurs and others in search of capital.

"There is a lot of money available today if an idea is valid," Nicholas said. "Minorities also have a good shot at this money."

San Francisco Chronicle

Business World

44   SATURDAY, JANUARY 12, 1974   ★★

Money Games

Old American Spirit Lives

By Sidney P. Allen
Financial Editor

A T THIS particular point in time you might suspect that the old American initiative was flagging.

But it's not necessarily so.

Here's Ted Nicholas, one-time ice-cream and candyman, out thumping the drum for his handy book on "How to Form Your Own Corporation Without a Lawyer for Under $50."

The appeal to do-it-yourself is nearly universal in this era of high service charges. And the further prospect of avoiding the lawyer in a time when it seems like the legal profession is surely "inheriting the earth" has real attraction.

Author Nicholas goes into the advantages of incorporating, including tax and stock benefits. And he describes in layman terms how to proceed and provides tear-out forms, minutes, by-laws and the necessary like.

When the author takes his own counsel, it tends to make believers. Nicholas claims to have founded 18 corporations in diverse businesses — food, confectionery, real estate, machinery, and licensing — in his career. He now heads three personal corporations, including Enterprise Publishing Co., 1300 Market Street, Wilmington, Del., publisher of his book.

He reports, with pleasure, that his book sales, at $8.40, are up over 50,000 and that over 1000 new incorporations have resulted so far. The free enterprise spirit lives.

★ ★ ★

Page C8   THE SACRAMENTO BEE
            Wednesday, Dec. 5, 1973

It's Your Business

Delaware: Mecca For Corporations

By John Burns

THE STATE OF DELAWARE, with a population less than Sacramento County, is the legal address of 72,000 corporations. That comes to one corporation for every seven residents.

Figured another way, the Blue Hen State has 34 corporations per square mile.

Delaware, you see, is in the corporation business. Firms doing business outside the state are offered inducements to incorporate there and the Delaware Corporation Department is a busy place.

Fees and taxes from corporations are the state's second largest source of revenue, exceeded only by its income tax.

Author-businessman Ted Nicholas, who is in California to promote sales of his book, "How to Form Your Own Corporation Without a Lawyer For Under $50," recited some of Delaware's attractions:

—There is no minimum capital requirement for incorporation.

—One person can be the president, treasurer, secretary and board of directors; a real one-man gang.

—A person can form a corporation by mail and never visit the state.

—There is no corporation income tax for firms which are organized in Delaware but do not operate in the state. Shares of stock owned by persons outside the state are not subject to Delaware taxes.

Nicholas mentioned other more complex concessions which have led major corporations such as General Motors, IBM, Xerox and PepsiCo to fly the Delaware flag. These are covered in the book.

A RESIDENT OF SUBURBAN WILMINGTON, DEL., the 39-year-old Nicholas operated several businesses, including a chain of 30 ice cream parlors, and now heads an organization aptly named The Corporation Co.

One of the company's products is what he calls the "All-In-One Corporate Outfit" ($27.95). It consists of a binder for corporate records; sample minutes and bylaws for a Delaware corporation; twenty stock certificates printed to order; and a miniature pocket seal for reproducing the corporate emblem.

Anyone who incorporates in Delaware must have a mailing address there. Nicholas' company will, for a fee of $25 to $100 a year, provide the address, forward mail and perform assorted other services as the registered agent of the corporation.

Although General Motors and Xerox types are unlikely to buy his "How To Form Your Own Corporation" book, or buy the do-it-yourself binder, or hire him as registered agent, there apparently is a demand for the services.

He told us he is the registered agent for 1,050 corporations but quickly added some of them are "people operating businesses out of their home, women supplementing the family income, manufacturers' representatives — often there is only one person in the corporation."

Under certain circumstances there are tax advantages or other reasons that prompt an individual or group to incorporate. And if they decide to do so, said Nicholas, why not in Delaware?

ALTHOUGH THE TITLE of Nicholas' book is an eye-catcher, it could be misleading. True, one might be able to incorporate in Delaware for $42.50 but that is the state's minimum fee, applicable to a stock issue of 1,000 or fewer shares.

The minimum figure presupposes the incorporator is going to go it alone, with neither a lawyer nor a registered agent. Unless he has a relative or a willing friend in Delaware, the out of state resident who spurns paid help will be hard-put to provide a valid mailing address there.

Then there is the requirement of being registered in the state where the corporation is actually doing business. California, for example, requires so-called foreign corporations to qualify themselves at a minimum fee of about $450.

The author does not hide these actual or possible extra costs but anyone who is thinking of incorporating in Delaware should not skip any pages in the book. The volume contains removable blank forms to be completed by the applicant.

"How to Form Your Own Corporation Without a Lawyer" is published in a paperback edition priced at $8.40 including postage, and in hard cover at $12.95. The publisher is the Enterprise Publishing Co., 1300 Market St., Wilmington, Del. 19801.

A Los Angeles Herald-Examiner, Monday, December 3, 1973   C-9

DO-IT-YOURSELF INCORPORATING

By LARCH CODY
Herald-Examiner Staff Writer

After a young man spends 17 years forming 18 corporations in diverse small businesses, from food, confectionary, real estate, machinery and licensing, among others, what does he do next?

One thing could be to write a book advising people how to form a corporation, at the lowest possible cost, and without the services of a lawyer.

Which is precisely what Ted Nicholas did.

Since he was 22 year old, in Delaware, he worked as a small businessman in a variety of enterprises. Some were successes, some were failures.

"I learned more from the failures, than the successes," he says.

Having gained first-hand information in the business world, he decided there was a need for a book on incorporating, directed toward the small businessman, telling him the advantages of incorporating, including tax and stock benefits, how to operate anonymously and the advantages of incorporation in the state of Delaware, the friendliest state in the union to corporations.

Visiting Los Angeles during a nation-wide promotion tour, even though his book has been through three printings and has been critically acclaimed by several small business associations and groups as well

Ted Nicholas

as individuals, Nicholas said the only group that is "less than enthusiastic" over his effort is the legal profession.

"In Texas, the bar association and the attorney general made an effort to stop the advertising of the book, but nothing has happened so far. My attorney said they had no right to stop the advertising, and we would fight if such an order was issued," he said.

The book, "How To Form Your Own Corporation Without A Lawyer For Under $50," is a step-by-step instructional manual for individuals who see an advantage in incorporating, including tear-out forms, certificates of incorporation, minutes, by-laws and other data necessary.

"Before this book was written, it was difficult for an individual to incorporate without a lawyer. There was no publication written in laymen's language. Also, companies who assist individuals in forming corporations usually work only through lawyers who prepare the documents. Legal fees therefore, were virtually unavoidable," said Nicholas.

Delaware is stressed as the state in which to incorporate. Mainly because of its low filing fees and easy tax laws toward corporations.

In conjunction with his instructions for forming corporations, he also has a corporation, in Delaware, which acts as an agent for would-be incorporators, for a small yearly fee.

Incidentally, Nicholas also owns the firm which publishes the book, as well as three other books on business subjects written by him.

Nicholas points out that do-it-yourself incorporation may not be for everyone, or for every business circumstance. He lists most of the occasions where incorporation is desirable and those circumstances where professional legal help is needed.

- 147 -

LEON HENRY, JR.—publisher

Home Office Report

A monthly roundup of news, ideas, time & money saving
hints to help you work at home more successfully.

VOL. V, No. 7, AUG. 1973

HOW TO FORM YOUR OWN CORPORATION WITHOUT A LAWYER FOR UNDER $50.00 has
been published by Enterprise Publishing Co., 2415 Allendale Rd.,
Wilmington, Delaware 19803. This report is written in layman's language
by Ted Nicholas, a businessman and business consultant. He explains
the advantages and the feasibility of incorporating, even for a one-man
business with little or no capital. Tear-out forms that are necessary

to forming a corporation are included in the book, complete with detailed
instructions.

Until now, it has been difficult for an individual to incorporate without
a lawyer whose fee could range from $200 to $1,000 or more. The author
of this book proves, however, that incorporation is a relatively simple
task that does not require professional services. Anyone in the United
States can take advantage of this formula as well as gain other money saving
and tax saving ideas. For a copy of the book, send $7.95, plus 45¢ to
cover postage, to the publisher.

Restaurant News

Volume IX Number 5
May 1974

Learn The Secrets of Raising Money

A new book called "WHERE THE MONEY IS AND HOW TO GET IT" has just been released by Enterprise Publishing Company in Wilmington, Delaware. this comprehensive detailed manual has been written by Ted Nicholas, the author of the best selling book "HOW TO FORM A CORPORATION WITHOUT A LAWYER FOR UNDER $50.00.

In 1964 Ted Nicholas was selected as one of the most outstanding businessmen in the nation and was invited to the White House to confer with the late Lyndon Johnson, President of the United States.

"WHERE THE MONEY IS AND HOW TO GET IT" could easily be worth its weight in diamonds to anyone who reads it and uses its ideas.

Over 2,000 money sources are listed in this book plus it contains valuable time saving tips such as ... How to Approach Any Capital Source. The Difference Between Venture and Adventure Capital, How to Get Long Term Financing, How to Use Other Peoples Money, How to Conduct a Stock Offering, plus dozens of other valuable ideas.

This comprehensive manual is "must" reading for anyone seeking capital for a new business (or business idea), scholarship funds, or a research grant, etc. The price of this unusual book is only $10.00 each, postage paid. It is hard bound and makes a wonderful gift. It is available from ENTERPRISE PUBLISHING CO., 1000 Oakfield Lane, Wilmington, Delaware 19810. Each book comes with a 10 day money-back guarantee.

Page 9

American INDUSTRY

ESTABLISHED 1946

May, 1974

Secrets of raising money

A new book called "Where The Money Is And How To Get It" is a comprehensive detailed manual written by Ted Nicholas, the author of the best selling book "How To Form A Corporation Without A Lawyer for Under $50.00". "Where The Money Is And How To Get It" could easily be worth its weight in diamonds to anyone who reads it and uses its ideas, according to publisher. More than 2,000 money sources are listed in this book plus it contains valuable time saving tips  such as; "How to Approach Any Capital Source," "The Difference Between Venture and Adventure Capital," "How to get Long Term Financing," "How to Use Other Peoples Money," "How to Conduct a Stock Offering," and dozens of other valuable ideas. Cost: $10.00, postage paid.

For details or copy write Enterprise Publishing Co., 1000 Oakfield Lane, Wilmington, Del. 19810, or use reader service coupon, identifying with No. 534.

ARTISTS AND ART SERVICES

Mrs. Sophie Adler
350 W. 31 St.
New York,N.Y. 10001
Tel: 212-594-5374
Book & jacket design, layout,
letterheads, lettering.

Miss Margaret Ayer
18492 Capricorn Court
Castro Valley,Ca.94546
Tel: 415-537-2377
Book illustration, color, line,
overlay. Special knowledge of
Orient, children, animals,
historical research.

Barbini, Pesce & Noble
110 E. 59 St.
New York,N.Y.10022
Tel: 212-688-5663
Complete art studio services
including preparation of brochures,
slides, mailing pieces, book &
jacket design, exhibit design,
letterheads, trademarks.

Volney Croswell, Jr.
791 Tremont St.
Boston,Mass. 02118
Tel: 617-266-4106
Book & jacket design, letterheads
and layout.

Liz Dauber
20 Farm Lane
Roosevelt,N.J.08555
Tel: 609-448-2320
Illustration, jacket design,
spot drawings.

Design Element
8624 Wonderland Ave.
Los Angeles,Ca.90046
Tel: 213-656-3293
Book,Jacket & poster design,
exhibit & map design,
cartoons, illustration,
letterheads, spot drawings,
trademarks; photography,
brochures, charts & graphs.

Adrianne Onderdonk Dudden
829 Old Gulph Rd.
Bryn Mawr,Pa. 19010
Tel: 215-525-6584
Book & jacket design,
illustration. Trade, text,
and art books.

John D.Firestone & Assoc.,Inc.
119 W.Waterloo St.
Canal Winchester,Ohio 43110
Tel: 614-837-4680, 837-5396
Book & jacket design,
illustraion, spot drawing,
complete production of
educational programs.

W. Kenneth Frederick
Godfrey Rd., East Thetford,
                    Vt. 05043
Tel: 802-785-2032
Book & jacket design, letter-
heads, trademarks.

Gary Gore
6551 Jocelyn Hollow Rd.
Nashville, Tenn. 37205
Tel: 615-352-1987
Book & jacket design, layout,
trademarks. Specialist in
scholarly & technical books.

Artists and Art Services-cont'd.

Philip Grushkin, Inc.
86 E. Linden Ave.
Englewood,N.J.07631
Tel: 201-568-6686
Book & jacket design, layout,
letterheads, lettering, trademarks, calligraphy, map & poster
design, complete production.

George Lenox
1438 Circle Ridge
Austin, Tex. 78746
Tel: 512-327-3183
Complete design, layout &
production for books, jackets,
posters, promotional pieces,
trademarks & corporate graphics.
Manufacturing sources in Asia.

Christo M. Popoff
R.R. 5, Box 451
East Lake Dr.
Edwardsville,Ill. 62025
Tel: 618-656-5577
Medical & scientific illustrations
& cartoons, film animation, poster
design, jacket design, lettering.

Repro Art Service
102 Swinick Dr.
Dunmore, Pa. 18512
Tel: 717-961-5410
Dir. Angelo Rinaldi
Assoc.Dir. John A. Wargo
Book & jacket design, retouching,
spot drawings, trademarks,
illustration, dummying, layout &
mechanicals, audiovisual.

Lenore Scott
4385 N.W. Malhuer St.
Portland, Ore. 97229
Tel: 503-645-2828
Layouts, designs, type specs,
letterheads, jackets, direct mail,
posters, pamphlets, mechanicals ready
for camera, books & ads.

Kelly Solis-Navarro
1051 Santa Cruz Ave.
Menlo Park,Ca.94025
Tel: 415-322-6937
Book, exhibit, jacket &
poster design, illustration,
layout, letterheads, lettering,
retouching, spot drawings,
trademarks, charts & graphs.

Vincent Torre
300 Central Park, W.
New York, N.Y.10024
Tel: 212-362-8469
Book, jacket & map design,
layout, lettering, spot
drawings.

Two One Two Limited
11 S. Foushee St.
Richmond, Va. 23220
Tel: 804-644-5448
Book, jacket & poster design,
cartoons, illustration, spot
drawings, letterheads,
trademarks, exhibit design,
film animation.

Visual Art Associates,Inc.
111-1275 Rd.
Forest Hills, N.Y.11375
Tel: 212-544-6262
Book, jacket, map & poster
design, illustration,
layout, letterheads,pictorial
statistics, retouching,
spot drawings, trademarks,
complete production.

Mrs. Lili Cassel Wronker
144-44 Village Rd.
Jamaica, N.Y. 11435
Tel: 212-380-3990
Illustration, jacket, map &
poster design, layout,
letterheads, lettering, spot
drawings, trademarks,
typography, photography.

BOOK REVIEW SERVICES

In addition to meeting the legal obligation to send to the Register of Copyrights, Washington, D.C. 20540, two copies of every book copyrighted in the U.S.A., it is customary to send additional copies (even where copyright is not claimed) to the following three places: The Library of Congress, Card Div., Dept. PWLC, Washington, D.C. 20541; "Weekly Record" Dept., Current Bibliography, 1180 Avenue of the Americas, New York, 10036; and the "Cumulative Book Index", c/o H. W. Wilson Co., 950 University Ave., Bronx, N.Y. 10452. These copies are sent, not on the chance of a review, but in the certainty of a listing. They are sent as early as possible (as finished books,) however, not as proofs) as a means of getting the book on public record in the National Union Catalog, the "Weekly Record" (and its monthly & annual "American Book Publishing Record") and the "Cumulative Book Index."

AB Bookman's Weekly
Box 1100, Newark, N.J. 07101
Tel: 201-MA 4-4454

American Classical Review
City University of N.Y.
Queens College,
Flushing, N.Y. 11367
Tel: 212-520-7546, 7164

Appraisal: Children's
Science Books
Children's Science Bk.
Review Comm.
Longfellow Hall
13 Appian Way,
Cambridge, Mass. 02138

Best-In-Books
416 N. Ridge Ave.
Rockwood, Tenn. 37854
Tel: 615-354-9033

Best Sellers
Univ. of Scranton Library
Scranton, Pa. 18510
Tel: 717-347-3321

Book Review Digest
H. W. Wilson Co.
950 University Ave.
Bronx, N.Y. 10452
Tel: 212-588-8400

The Booklist
American Library Assn.
50 E. Huron St.
Chicago, Ill. 60611
Tel: 312-944-6780

Bulletin of the Center for
Children's Books
1100 E. 57th St.
Chicago, Ill. 60637
Tel: 312-753-3450

CAS Review
Pub. by Curriculum Advisory Service
500 S. Clinton St.
Chicago, Ill. 60607
Tel: 312-939-1333

Choice
Assoc. of College & Research Libraries
ALA, 100 Riverview Center
Middletown, Conn. 06457
Tel: 203-347-6933

Book Review Services - cont'd

The Horn Book Magazine
Horn Book, Inc.
585 Boylston St.
Boston, Mass. 02116
Tel: 617-536-3145

Insurance Literature
Special Libraries Assoc.
Insurance Div.
c/o Life Insurance Agency Management
Assoc., 170 Sigourney St.
Hartford, Conn. 06105
Tel: 203-525-0881

Jewish Book Council of the
National Jewish Welfare Board
15 E. 26 St.
New York, N.Y. 10010
Tel: 212-532-4949

The Kirkus Review
60 W. 13 St.
New York, N.Y. 10011
Tel: 212-929-7997

Kliatt Paperback Book Guide
6 Crocker Circle
West Newton, Mass. 02165
Tel: 617-969-6499

Law Books in Review
Glanville Publishers,Inc.
Dobbs Ferry, N.Y. 10522
Tel: 914-693-1394

Library Journal-The Book Review
1180 Ave. of the Americas
New York, N.Y. 10036
Tel: 212-764-5100

Medievalia Et Humanistica
Box 13348, N.Tex. State Univ.
Denton, Tex. 76203
Tel: 817-788-2101

The Mensa Bulletin
50 E. 42 St.
New York, N.Y. 10017
Tel: 212-687-0037

New York Review of Books
250 W. 57th St.
New York, N.Y. 10019
Tel: 212-PL 7-8070

Pacific Search
715 Harrison St.
Seattle, Wash. 98109
Tel: 206-682-5044

Publishers Weekly-Forecasts
1180 Ave. of the Americas
New York, N.Y. 10036
Tel: 212-764-5100

Reprint Bulletin-Book Reviews
Glanville Publishers,Inc.
Dobbs Ferry, N.Y. 10522
Tel: 914-693-1394

The Review of Books & Religion
Box 86, White River Junction,
Vt. 05001
Tel: 802-295-5323

The Review of Education
Redgrave Information Resources Corp.
53 Wilton Rd.
Westport, Conn. 06880
Tel: 203-226-9523

Reviews in American History
Redgrave Information Resources Corp.
53 Wilton Rd.
Westport, Conn. 06880
Tel: 203-226-9523

Book Review Services - cont'd.

Reviews in Anthropology
Redgrave Information Resources Corp.
53 Wilton Rd.
Westport, Conn. 06880
Tel: 203-226-9523

Reviews in European History
Redgrave Information Resources Corp.
53 Wilton Rd.
Westport, Conn. 06880
Tel: 203-226-9523

Reviews on Cards-Library Journal
School Library Journal
1180 Ave. of the Americas
New York, N.Y. 10036
Tel: 212-764-5100

SFRA Newsletter
3608 Meadow Oaks Lane
Bryan, Tex. 77801
Tel: 713-845-6211, ext. 20

School Library Journal
The Book Review
1180 Ave. of the Americas
New York, N.Y. 10036
Tel: 212-764-5100

Science Reviews: Books & Films
American Assn. for the
Advancement of Science
1515 Massachusetts Ave.NW
Washington,D.C. 20005
Tel: 202-467-4400

Sighted From the Crows-Nest
2820 W. Dravus St.
Seattle, Wash. 98199
Tel: 206-AT 3-7233

Speaking Personally
500 E. 77 St.
New York, N.Y. 10021
Tel: 212-861-9567

Tartan Book Sales Catalog
1609 Memorial Ave.
Williamsport, Pa. 17701
Tel: 717-326-2461

Technical Book Review Index
Special Libraries Assn.
235 Park Ave. S.
New York, N.Y. 10003
Tel: 212-777-8136

University Review (UR)
857 Broadway
New York, N.Y. 10003
Tel: 212-255-2048

Western Letter
San Francisco Book Co.,Inc.
681 Market St., Rm. 244
San Francisco, Ca. 94105
Tel: 415-922-1033

Charles W. White
107 Audubon Dr., P.O. 338
Carmel, Ind. 46032
Tel: 317-846-8508

World Wide News Bureau
309 Varick St.
Jersey City, N.J. 07302
Tel: 201-333-4660

BOOK REVIEW SYNDICATES

AP Newsfeatures
50 Rockefeller Plaza
New York, N.Y. 10020
Tel: 212-262-4094

Allan's Galley
RFD 2, Zames St.
Derry, N.H. 03038
Tel: 603-432-2614

John Barkham Reviews
27 E. 65 St
New York, N.Y. 10021
Tel: 212-TR-9-9705

John E. Drewry
Henry W. Grady,
School of Journalism
Univ. of Georgia
Athens, Ga. 30601
Tel: 404-542-4466

Feature News Service
2330 S. Brentwood Blvd.
St. Louis, Mo. 63144
Tel: 314-961-9825

Edwin T. Grandy's Syndicated
Book Reviews
Box 339, Route 17
Mill Valley, Calif. 94941

King Features Syndicate
235 E. 45 St.
New York, New York 10017
Tel: 212-MU 2-5600

Charles Lee
Presidential Apts. D-1203
Phila., Pa. 19131
Tel: 215-GR 3-2188

Jeffrey Lee Syndicate
2 Holly Dr.
New Rochelle, N.Y. 10801
Tel: 914-BE 5-2347

The Literary Lantern
418 Whitehead Cir.
Chapel Hill, N.C. 27514
Tel: 919-968-3087

Mid-Continent Feature Syndicate
Box 1662
Pittsburgh, Pa. 15230
Tel: 412-261-5307

Miss Beatrice M. Murphy
117 R St., N.E.
Washington, D.C. 20002
Tel: 202-635-9084

National Catholic News Service
1312 Massachusetts Ave. NW
Washington, D.C. 20005
Tel: 202-659-6722

North American Newspaper Alliance
220 E. 42 St.
New York, N.Y. 10017
Tel: 212-682-3020

Register & Tribune Syndicate
715 Locust St.
Des Moines, Iowa 50304
Tel: 515-284-8244

George H. Tweney
16660 Marine View Dr., S.W.
Seattle, Wash. 98166
Tel: 206-243-8243

United Press International
220 E. 42 St., New York 10017
Tel: 212-MU 2-0400

World-Wide News Bureau
309 Varick St.
Jersey City, N.J. 07302
Tel: 201-333-4660

COURSES FOR THE BOOK TRADE

Various courses are given each year covering different phases of the book trade and graphic arts. Among the institutions and associations sponsoring such courses are the ones listed below. Detailed information can be obtained by writing directly to the universities or associations.

Columbia University
Writing Div., School of the Arts
404 Dodge.
Columbia Univ., N.Y. 10027
Tel: 212-280-4391
Graduate writing program. Two-year course leading to the M.F.A. degree. Seminars in poetry, fiction, nonfiction & translation.

Federal Bar Council
26 W. 56th St.
New York, N.Y. 10019
Tel: 212-247-7190

Graphic Arts Education Center
Graphic Arts Assn. of
Delaware Valley, Inc.
1900 Cherry St., Phila., Pa.19103
Tel: 215-LO 7-3211

Harvard Summer School
Radcliffe's Course in Publishing Procedures.
10 Garden St.,
Cambridge, Mass. 02138
Tel: 617-495-8678

Hunter College
School of General Studies
(Adult Education Programs
Center for Lifelong Learning)
695 Park Ave., New York 10021
Tel: 212-BU 8-7210, 360-2170

Institute of Early American
History & Culture
Box 220, Williamsburg, Va. 23185
Tel: 804-229-2771

Los Angeles City College
855 N. Vermont Ave.
Los Angeles, Calif. 90029
Tel: 213-663-9141

Mystery Writers of America
105 E. 19th St.
New York, N.Y. 10003
Tel: 212-473-8020

New School for Social Research
66 W. 12th St.
New York, N.Y. 10011
Tel: 212-OR-5-2700

New York City Community College
Graphic Arts & Advertising Technology
300 Jay St.
Brooklyn, N.Y. 11201
Tel: 212-643-8595

New York University
School of Continuing Education
2 University Place
New York, N.Y. 10003
Tel: 212-598-2373

Northwestern University
Medill School of Journalism
Fisk Hall,
1845 Sheridan Rd.
Evanston, Ill. 60201
Tel: 312-492-5571

Courses for the Book Trade - cont'd.

Ohio University
English Dept.
Creative Writing Program
Athens, Ohio 45701
Tel: 614-594-5511

Printing Industries of
Metropolitan New York, Inc
461 Eighth Ave.
New York, N.Y.10001
Tel: 212-LO 4-3500

Rochester Institute of
Technology
School of Printing
Rochester, N.Y. 14623
Tel: 716-464-2727

School of Visual Arts
Admission-Day & Evening School
209 E. 23 St.
New York, N.Y. 10010
Tel: 212-679-7350

Simmons College
300 The Fenway
Boston, Mass. 02115
Tel: 617-738-2264

Syracuse University
School of Public Communications
Syracuse, N.Y. 13210
Tel: 315-GR 6-5571, Est. 2301

University of Wisconsin Extension
Journalism & Mass Communication Dept.
221 Lowell Hall
610 Langdon St.
Madison, Wis. 53706
Tel: 608-262-3982

DIRECT MAIL SPECIALISTS

Accurate Mail/Marketing Corp.
32-02 Queens Blvd.
Long Island City, N.Y. 11101
Tel: 212-786-7600

Ahrend Associates, Inc.
64 University Place
New York, N.Y. 10003
Tel: 212-533-1640

Muriel Atkinson
59 W. 12th St.
New York, N.Y. 10011
Tel: 212-924-0935

Automatic Typewritten
Letters Corp.
See Dezer Productions,Inc.

Barbini, Pesce & Noble
110 E. 59 St.
New York, N.Y. 10022
Tel: 212-688-5663

Beaumont-Bennett, Inc.
605 Third Ave.
New York, N.Y. 10016
Tel: 212-573-8450

The Beverly Bond Group
800 West End Ave.
New York, N.Y. 10025
Tel: 212-UN 6-2914

Ray Boultinghouse, Inc.
475 Park Ave. S.
New York, N.Y. 10016
Tel: 212-679-7950

Richard Buehrer Assoc., Inc.
Dept. MC, 347 Mineola Blvd.
Mineola, N.Y. 11501
Tel: 516-248-3651

Copy, Etc.
15 Golden Ct.
Cromwell, Conn. 06416
Tel: 203-635-1502

Curriculum Information Center, Inc.
1020 15 St, Brooks Towers,
Suite 42-C, Denver, Colo. 80202
Tel: 303-573-7167

Dezer Productions, Inc.
122 E. 42 St.
New York, N.Y. 10017
Tel: 212-661-8616

Direct Mail Promotions, Inc.
Co-operative Mailing Div.
342 Madison Ave.
New York, N.Y. 10017
Tel: 212-687-1910

Distribution Systems, Inc.
460 Howell St.
Bristol, Pa. 19007
Tel: 215-785-3581

George Feldman
Advertising/Marketing Consultants
15 W. 38th St., New York 10018
Tel: 212-279-3660

(Flex) Free Lance Exchange, Inc.
342 Madison Ave.
New York, N.Y. 10017
Tel: 212-682-3042

Hibbert Company
21 Muirhead Ave.
Trenton, N.J. 08607
Tel: 609-394-7500

Holub + Associates
432 Park Ave. S., New York 10016
Tel: 212-889-6626

Direct Mail Specialists - Cont'd.

Laurence Jaeger
277 Park Place
Brooklyn, N.Y. 11238
Tel: 212-783-0992

Januz Direct Marketing Corp.
3553 W. Peterson Ave.
Chicago, Ill. 60659
Tel: 312-583-8660

KRC Associates
105 Wagner Ave.
Mamaroneck, N.Y. 10543
Tel: 914-698-3855

Kameny, Solomon, Sherwood &
Partners, Inc.
110 E. 59th St.
New York, N.Y. 10022
Tel: 212-HA 1-5522

Dorothy Kerr & Associates
1211 Connecticut Ave. NW
Washington, D.C. 20036
Tel: 202-296-1478

Lankenau Associates, Advertising
Box 1261
Indianapolis, Ind. 46206
Tel: 317-251-7812

Michael Larsen/Elizabeth Pomada
1029 Jones St.
San Francisco, Calif. 94109
Tel: 415-673-0939

Lorrie Lewis & Associates
956 Fifth Ave.
New York, N.Y. 10021
Tel: 212-628-3972

MZA Advertising, Inc.
331 Madison Ave., New York 10017
Tel: 212-682-1280

Mail Marketing Services
Box 1042
Kansas City, Mo. 64141
Tel: 816-931-6170

Market Data Retrieval
800 Boxton Post Rd.
Westport, Conn. 06880
Tel: 203-226-7358

Mediaprint, Inc.
12 W. 18th St.
New York, N.Y. 10011
Tel: 212-YU 2-7777

Miro Packaging Corp.
Chatham-Phoenix Bldg.
29-28 41 St.
Long Island City, N.Y. 11101
Tel: 212-729-0536

Paul Muchnick Company
1560 Saltair Ave.
Los Angeles, Calif. 90025
Tel: 213-826-0457

Murphy O'Hagan Coordinated
Communications
110 E. 87th St.
New York, N.Y. 10028
Tel: 212-427-0263

Elizabeth Pomada
See Michael Larsen

Ramer/Wolsk Associates, Inc.
509 Madison Ave.
New York, N.Y. 10022

Reply-O-Letter Co., Inc.
1860 Broadway, New York 10023
Tel: 212-245-8118'

Response Group, Inc.
39 Pine Dr.
Park Ridge, N.J. 07656
Tel: 201-391-8820,NYC 752-2320

Direct Mail Specialists - Cont'd.

Richardson Associates
25 Walker Place
Albertson, N.Y. 11507
Tel: 516-248-5741

Alan H. Rosenberg Assoc.,Inc.
350 Fifth Ave.
New York, N.Y. 10001
Tel: 212-564-7140

Sales Letters, Inc.
(subsidiary of ALCO INDUSTRIES)
307 W. 36th St., N.Y. 10018
Tel: 212-279-4800

Schecterson & Schecterson
6 E. 39th St.
New York, N.Y. 10016
Tel: 212-889-3950

J.J. Spector & Associates
2900 N.E. 30th St.
Ft. Lauderdale, Fla. 33306
Tel: 305-563-4093

William Steiner Associates, Inc
527 Madison Ave
New York, N.Y. 10022
Tel: 212-688-7030

Twain Associates
Box 1179
Lowell, Mass. 01853
Tel: 617-453-5944

Unicorn Promotion
2 Fifth Ave., Apt. 16G
New York, N.Y. 10011
Tel: 212-673-5717

Michael C. Wales & Company
211 W. Madison St.
South Bend, Ind. 46601
Tel: 219-232-4200; 234-0131

BOOK MANUFACTURERS

Adams Press
30 W. Washington St.
Chicago, Ill. 60602
Tel: 312-CE 6-3838

Alpine Press
Alpine Dr.
S. Braintree, Mass. 02185
Tel: 617-848-1600

American Photoengraving Co.,Inc.
66 N. Juniper St.
Philadelphia, Pa. 19107
Tel: 215-LO 4-0400

Anderson, Ritchie & Simon
3044 Riverside Dr.
Los Angeles, Calif. 90039
Tel: 213-664-2181

Arcata Book Group
Box 191
Kingsport, Tenn. 37662
Tel: 615-246-8147

George Banta Company, Inc.
Menasha, Wis. 54952
Tel: 414-722-7771

Beck Engraving Co., Inc.
22 E. 49th St.
New York, N.Y. 10017
Tel: 212-832-2020

The Book Press
Div. of General Educational
Services Corp.
Plant: Putney Rd.
Brattleboro, Vt. 05301
Tel: 802-257-7701

Book Reprint Service
1536-40 N. 59th St.
Phila., Pa. 19151
Tel: 215-477-9100

The R. L. Bryan Company
Box 368 Greystone Executive Park
Columbia, S.C. 29202
Tel: 803-779-3560

Challenge Printing Company
8 Hathaway St.
Wallington, N.J. 07057
Tel: 201-471-4700

Colorton Press
Colortone Bldg.
2400 17 St.,N.W.
Washington, D.C. 20009
Tel: 202-DY 7-6800

Creative Book Services
Div. of McGregor & Werner, Inc.
15 E. 40th St.
New York, N.Y. 10016
Tel: 212-686-5810

John H. Dekker & Sons, Inc.
2941 Clydon St., S.W.
Grand Rapids, Mich. 49509
Tel: 616-538-5160

R. R. Donnelly & Sons Co.
2223 Martin Luther King Dr.
Chicago, Ill. 60616
Tel: 312-326-8000

Exposition Press, Inc.
900 S. Oyster Bay Rd.
Hicksville, N.Y. 11801
Tel: 516-822-5700

The William Feather Company
Copifyer Div.
9900 Clinton Rd.
Cleveland, Ohio 44144
Tel: 216-281-4122

Graphic Composition, Inc.
240 Hawthorne Ave.
Athens, Ga. 30601
Tel: 404-546-8688

Book Manufacturers - cont'd.

A. Hoen & Co., Inc.
Lithographers & Printers
Chester Chase & Biddle Sts.
Baltimore, Md. 21213
Tel: 301-732-6510

International Graphics, Inc.
2901 Simms St.
Hollywood, Fla. 33020
Tel: 305-927-1717

Josten's American Yearbook Co.
4000 Adams, Topeka, Kans. 66609
Tel: 913-266-3300

Kingsport Press
see Arcata Book Group

W. A. Krueger Co.
7301 E. Helm Dr.
Scottsdale, Ariz. 85260
Tel: 602-948-5650

The Maple Press Co., Inc.
210-240 E. York St.
York, Pa 17403
Tel: 717-764-5911

Moran Industries, Inc.
5425 Florida Blvd.
Baton Rouge, La. 70806
Tel: 504-924-6281

Lorrin L. Morrison
Printer & Publisher
1915 S. Western Ave.
Los Angeles, Calif. 90018
Tel: 213-734-1911

√ Multiprint, Inc.
28 W. 23 St.
New York, N.Y. 10010
Tel: 212-924-1103

Pantagraph Printing & Stationery Co.
217 W. Jefferson St.
Bloomington, Ill. 61701
Tel: 309-829-1071

Parker & Son, Inc.
6500 Flotilla St.
Los Angeles, Calif. 90022
Tel: 213-724-6622

Publishers' Book Bindery, Inc.
21 East St.
Winchester, Mass. 01890
Tel: 617-729-8000

Quinn & Boden Co., Inc.
1905 Elizabeth Ave.
Rahway, N.J. 07065
Tel: 201-FU 8-0216

Recorder-Sunset Press
99 S. Van Ness Ave.
San Francisco, Calif. 94103
Tel: 415-621-5400

Rose Printing Co., Inc.
2503 Jackson Bluff Rd., Box 5078
Tallahassee, Fla. 32301
Tel: 904-576-4151

Sharp Offset Printing, Inc.
10-12 Cleveland Ave.
Rutland, Vt. 05701
Tel: 802-773-9194

Smith-Edwards-Dunlap Co.
Allegheny Ave. at Del. Expwy
Phila., Pa. 19134
Tel: 215-GA 5-8800

Sultana Press/Premier Printing Corp.
124 W. Wilshire Ave
Fullerton, Calif. 92632
Tel: 714-871-3121; 213-691-4133

Book Manufacturers - cont'd.

Taylor Publishing Company
1550 W. Mockingbird La.,
Box 597, Dallas, Tex. 75221
Tel: 214-637-2800

The Telegraph Press
Box 1831, Cameron & Kelker St.
Harrisburg, Pa. 17105
Tel: 717-234-5091

United Printing Services, Inc.   ✓
263 Chapel St.
New Haven, Conn. 06513
Tel: 203-562-3101

Velo-Bind Press
Sunnyvale, Calif. 94086

Vicks Lithograph & Printing Corp.
Commercial Dr.
Yorkville, N.Y. 13495
Tel: 315-736-9346

Von-Hoffman Press, Inc.
1000 Camera Ave.
St. Louis, Mo. 63126
Tel: 314-966-0909

The Webb Company
1999 Shepard Rd.
St. Paul, Minn. 55116
Tel: 612-647-7200

Western Publishing Co., Inc.
1220 Mound Ave.
Racine, Wis. 53404
Tel: 414-633-2431

Wickersham Printing Co.
111 E. Chestnut St.
Lancaster, Pa. 17604
Tel: 717-393-3989

WHOLESALERS TO BOOK STORES

A & A Distributors, Inc.
Mear Road
Holbrook, MA 02343
Tel: 617-767-3000
Irwin S. Miller
Aaron Rabinovitz

Ancorp National Services, Inc.
34 Hubert Street
New York, NY 10013
Tel: 212-925-5642
Vice President & Book Buyer
Joseph M. Christie

The Baker & Taylor Co.
A Division of W. R. Grace & Co.
Exec. Off: 6 Kirby Avenue
Somerville, NJ 08876
Tel: 201-526-8000
President: Jack D. Willis
Corp. Cont: Kenneth Goelz
Dir., Mktg. & Sales: Fred A. Philipp
New Book Buyer: William E. Boyer
  Tel: 201-722-8000
Eastern Division:
  50 Kirby Avenue
  Somerville, NJ 08876
  Tel: 201-722-8000
  V. Pres. & Gen. Mgr.: William
    J. Saller, Jr.
Midwest Division:
  Gladiola Avenue
  Momence, IL 60954
  Tel: 815-472-2444
  V. Pres. & Gen. Mgr.: Richard L.
    Porter
Southeast Division:
  Commerce, GA 30529
  Tel: 404-335-5000
  V. Pres. & Gen. Mgr.: Richard S.
    Blue
Southwest Division:
  Industrial Park
  Clarksville, TX 75426
  Tel: 214-427-3811
  V. Pres. & Gen. Mgr.: Leslie M
    Schneyder

Western Division:
  380 Edison Way
  Reno, NV 89502
  Tel: 702-786-6700
  V. Pres. & Gen Mgr.: Harold C.
    Sexton

Book Jobbers Hawaii, Inc.
805 S. Queen Street
Honolulu, Hawaii 96813
Tel: 808-533-1070; 3072
Gen. Mgr.: William B. Stull

Bookazine Co., Inc.
303 W. 10 Street
New York, NY 10017
Tel: 212-675-8877
Pres.: William Epstein

Bookpeople, Inc.
2940 Seventh Street
Berkeley, CA 94710
Tel: 415-549-3033
Pres.: Miriam Foley

Campbell and Hall - Booksmith
Distributing Co.
Division of Learning Resources, Inc.
1075 Commonwealth Avenue
Boston, MA 02117
Tel: 617-254-4500
Gen. Mgr.: Marshall J. Smith

De Vorss & Co., Inc.
1641 Lincoln Boulevard
Santa Monica, CA 90404
Tel: 213-451-0660

DeWolfe & Fiske, Inc.
Pequot Industrial Park
300 Turnpike Street
Canton, MA 02021
Tel: 617-828-8300
Mgr.: George Townson

Wholesalers To Book Stores - cont'd.

Dimondstein Book Co., Inc.
38 Portman Road
New Rochelle, NY 10801
Tel: 914-NE6-6000
Pres.: Herbert Dimondstein

Ingram Book Company
347 Reedwood Drive
Nashville, TN 37217
Tel: 615-889-1104

Inland Book Distributors
642 Facotry Road
Addison, IL 60101
Tel: 312-626-4060

International Publications Service
114 E. 32 Street
New York, NY 10016
Rel: 212-685-9351
Gen. Mgr.: William C. Collings

International Service Company
333 Fourth Avenue
Indialantic, FL 32903
Tel: 305-724-1443
Pres.: Dennis Samuels

Milligan News Co., Inc.
150 N. Autumn Street
San Jose, CA 96110
Tel: 408-286-7604

Raymar Book Company
1551 S. Primrose Avenue
Monrovia, CA 91016
Tel: 213-358-1801
Stuart Woodruff, Frnacis Howell

Research Services Corp.
5280 Trail Lake Drive
Fort Worth, TX 76133
Tel: 817-292-4270
Eastern Division:
   801 Asbury Avenue
   Drawer 540
   Ocean City, NJ 08226
   Tel: 609-399-7066

Wellington Book Co., Inc.
33-49 Whelan Road
East Rutherford, NJ 07073
Tel: 201-933-8300
Pres.: Richard Wellington

World Book Import & Export, Inc.
51 E. 73 Street
New York, NY 10021
Tel: 212-988-2546
Pres.: Paul Anthony Ender

X-S Books, Inc.
100 Commerce Road
Carlstadt, NJ 07072
Tel: 201-935-4493
Pres.: Tom Eliopoulos

OTHER TOP SELLING PUBLICATIONS BY TED NICHOLAS
AND ENTERPRISE PUBLISHING COMPANY

1.   HOW TO SELF PUBLISH YOUR OWN BOOK & MAKE IT A BEST SELLER
              ($14.95 plus 45¢ postage & handling)
     In this how-to-do-it manual Ted Nicholas describes how he
     has become a best selling author with sales of over 100,000
     copies of his very first book by publishing it himself.
     If you have written or thought about writing a book, you will
     learn how to publish it yourself to maximize profit and maintain
     control over distribution and sales. Simplified step by step
     procedure shows you how it is possible to see your work in
     print for surprisingly little cost.

2.   DON'T BE AFRAID-START YOUR OWN BUSINESS
              (Cassette Tape - $14.95 postpaid)
     74 minute seminar given live! Hear Ted Nicholas describe
     exactly step by step how to start a business. Learn how to
     begin it with zero capital. Ideas for business opportunities
     that can be started part time. How to raise capital if
     needed. What types of business actually benefit from recession
     and inflation. Given before a high school audience but
     applicable to any present or would-be entrepeneur.

3.   HOW TO GET OUT IF YOU'RE IN OVER YOUR HEAD
              ($9.95 plus 45¢ postage & handling)
     How to handle your debts and deal with creditors. Myths about
     bankruptcy exploded. Even the social stigma of failure can be
     avoided. How to avoid bankruptcy. Determine when it is the
     best solution. Discover how you either personally or with
     your business can utilize the bankruptcy laws to your advantage
     the way big corporations have for years. Information never
     before revealed. How to exclude from bankruptcy proceedings
     more assets than you would imagine, up to $40,000!

4.   AM - HOW TO TEACH YOURSELF MEDITATION
              ($9.95 plus 45¢ postage & handling)
     A new way to release tension and achieve more of your creative
     potential. (Anthrocentric means "man centered.") This
     relaxation technique considers man to be the center of the
     universe. Methods can be learned in one evening. Just two 15
     minute periods a day give you deeper form of rest than sleep and
     at the same time enhance your creative powers. You'll feel
     better and even look better. All the secrets revealed. People
     are meditating successfully all over the world, businessmen,
     students, housewives, etc. We absolutely guarantee you'll benefit!

5. LETTERS TO JOSEPH SELIGMAN AND RALPH NADER IN OPPOSITION TO
    FEDERAL INCORPORATION   ($2.00 postpaid)
    Ralph Nader is an advocate of federal incorporation, to replace
    the present system of each State having its own corporation
    department. His organization asked Ted Nicholas to assist him.
    Ted Nicholas believes we should have less government in our
    lives, not more. See his interesting answers in two open
    letters and learn why he considers this Nader idea potentially
    the forerunner to the loss of individual rights and possible
    fascism in the U.S. Anyone who loves individual freedom would
    benefit from this information.

6. HOW TO DO BUSINESS - TAX FREE -- by Midas Malone
                ($14.95 plus 45¢ postage & handling)
    By special arrangements we have obtained exclusive publishing
    and distribution rights from an overseas publisher to market
    this outstanding and authoritative work on tax havens. It is
    not only well written, it is packed with helpful information you
    can put to practical use. After researching every book available
    on the subject, we consider this to be the leading work on tax
    havens. Learn about how you as an individual citizen living
    in the U.S. or another country can arrange your affairs to
    legally pay little or no tax. Information includes who to
    contact and usable forms to help you get started. Sections
    on Switzerland, Hong Kong, Liechtenstein, Cayman Islands,
    Panama, Bahamas, Bermuda, Monaco, Ireland, etc. Over 15 of
    the major and minor tax havens of the world. Facts on setting
    up a trust or a corporation. Operate a business, buy or sell
    property, securities, silver and gold anywhere in the world--
    tax free in many instances!

7. HOW TO FORM YOUR OWN CORPORATION WITHOUT A LAWYER FOR UNDER $50
                ($9.95 plus 45¢ postage & handling)
    Number 1 runaway best seller. Complete with tear-out forms.
    Contains numerous money and tax saving ideas. Now in its sixth
    big printing. Fully revised with latest information. Over
    130,000 copies in print.

8. HOW TO FORM YOUR OWN CORPORATION WITHOUT A LAWYER FOR UNDER $50
                ($14.95 plus 45¢ postage & handling)
    Beautifully cloth bound 6th Limited Library edition with gold
    stamping. For your business library, a real collector's item.
    Practical and elegant for gift giving.

9. HOW AND WHERE TO RAISE VENTURE CAPITAL TO FINANCE A BUSINESS
                ($6.95 postpaid)
    227 sources of venture capital, classified by name, address,
    telephone number and individual to contact. Also includes
    information as to how to approach a capital source, and many
    of the author's personal experiences.

Page #3.

10. WHERE THE MONEY IS AND HOW TO GET IT
                    ($12.50 plus 45¢ postage & handling)
     How and where to raise capital for a business. Contains
     hundreds of sources of loans and venture capital. Includes
     names, addresses and phone numbers. Fully expanded list
     includes venture capital firms, state sources, and selected
     banks. Techniques save you time and produce results. A
     must for every business library.

11. HOW TO SET UP YOUR OWN MEDICAL REIMBURSEMENT PLAN
                    ($5.00 postpaid) (Printed in form of a report)
     Report shows how all medical and dental expenses are fully tax
     deductible. This includes prescription drugs and applies to a
     business owner and his family. Contains a blank form with
     instructions for completion. Can be made effective immediately.
     This eye opening report takes only a few minutes to read. This
     valuable tax angle is used by businessmen, small and large,
     throughout the nation. It has saved people thousands of dollars
     in taxes. Weeks of research condensed in a few pages.

          All publications sold with a 10 day money back guarantee.

ORDER FORM

TO: ENTERPRISE PUBLISHING CO.
     1300 Market Street, Dept. P
     Wilmington, DE. 19801

     Please send me the following publications: (Order by number please.)

	Qty.	Amount			Qty.	Amount
#1 @ $14.95	___	____	#7. @ $ 9.95		___	____
#2 @ 14.95	___	____	#8 @ 14.95		___	____
#3 @ 9.95	___	____	#9 @ 6.95		___	____
#4 @ 9.95	___	____	#10 @ 12.50		___	____
#5 @ 2.00	___	____	#11 @ 5.00		___	____
#6 @ 14.95	___	____	Plus postage & handling			____
			TOTAL ORDER			____

Special quantity discount when ordering: 3 or more publications
                                             deduct 10%
                                          6 or more publications
                                             deduct 20%

___ check enclosed ___ Master Charge ___ Carte Blanche
    ____ BankAmericard ____ Diner's Club

No. _____ Expiration Date _____

Signature _____

Name (Please print) _____

Address _____

City _____ State _____ Zip _____

IN A RUSH? CREDIT CARD ORDERS BY PHONE

Call 302-656-3174 and we will ship your order by special delivery or
air mail immediately. Sorry no collect calls or C.O.D.

Please have your credit card number and expiration date ready.

Phone order hours: Mon-Fri - 10 AM - 3 PM E.S.T.